An Assessment of the NIH Women's Health Initiative

Committee to Review the NIH
Women's Health Initiative

Food and Nutrition Board
and
Board on Health Sciences Policy

INSTITUTE OF MEDICINE

Susan Thaul and Dana Hotra, Editors

NATIONAL ACADEMY PRESS
Washington, D.C. 1993

NATIONAL ACADEMY PRESS • 2101 Constitution Avenue, N.W. • Washington, DC 20418

NOTICE: The project that is the subject of this report was approved by the Governing Board of the National Research Council, whose members are drawn from the councils of the National Academy of Sciences, the National Academy of Engineering, and the Institute of Medicine. The members of the committee responsible for the report were chosen for their special competences and with regard for appropriate balance.

This report has been reviewed by a group other than the authors according to procedures approved by a Report Review Committee consisting of members of the National Academy of Sciences, the National Academy of Engineering, and the Institute of Medicine.

The Institute of Medicine was chartered in 1970 by the National Academy of Sciences to enlist distinguished members of the appropriate professions in the examination of policy matters pertaining to the health of the public. In this, the Institute acts under both the Academy's 1863 congressional charter responsibility to be an adviser to the federal government and its own initiative in identifying issues of medical care, research, and education. Dr. Kenneth I. Shine is the president of the Institute of Medicine.

This study was supported by project no. NO1-WH-3-2114 from the National Institutes of Health.

Library of Congress Catalog Card No. 93-86833

International Standard Book Number 0-309-04989-X

Additional copies of this report are available for sale from:

National Academy Press
2101 Constitution Avenue, NW
Box 285
Washington, DC 20418

Call 800-624-6242 or 202-334-3313 (in the Washington Metropolitan Area).

B248

Copyright 1993 by the National Academy of Sciences. All rights reserved.

Printed in the United States of America

The serpent has been a symbol of long life, healing, and knowledge among almost all cultures and religions since the beginning of recorded history. The image adopted as a logotype by the Institute of Medicine is based on a relief carving from ancient Greece, now held by the Staatlichemuseen in Berlin.

COMMITTEE TO REVIEW THE NATIONAL INSTITUTES OF HEALTH WOMEN'S HEALTH INITIATIVE

MARION J. FINKEL (*Chair*), Sandoz Pharmaceuticals Corporation, East Hanover, New Jersey
LUCILE L. ADAMS-CAMPBELL, Howard University Cancer Center
ABDELMONEM A. AFIFI, University of California, Los Angeles
KELLY D. BROWNELL, Yale University
GARY R. CUTTER, Pythagoras, Inc., Birmingham, Alabama
JOHN W. FARQUHAR,[*] Stanford University School of Medicine
M.R.C. GREENWOOD,[*] University of California, Davis (Resigned July 7, 1993)
JENNIFER L. KELSEY, Stanford University School of Medicine
PENNY M. KRIS-ETHERTON, The Pennsylvania State University
JOANNE LYNN, Dartmouth Medical School
LYNN ROSENBERG, Slone Epidemiology Unit, Boston University School of Medicine
DIANE B. STOY, The George Washington University Medical Center

Staff

SUSAN THAUL, Study Director
DANA HOTRA, Research Associate
FELICE LePAR, Research Assistant
DONNA ALLEN, Project Assistant

[*] Member, Institute of Medicine

FOOD AND NUTRITION BOARD

M.R.C. GREENWOOD* (*Chair*), University of California, Davis
EDWIN L. BIERMAN* (*Vice Chair*), University of Washington School of Medicine
PERRY L. ADKISSON,* Department of Entomology, Texas A&M University
LINDSAY H. ALLEN, Nutritional Sciences, University of Connecticut
DENNIS M. BIER, Pediatric Endocrinology and Metabolism,
    Washington University School of Medicine
HECTOR F. DELUCA,[†] Department of Biochemistry, University of Wisconsin, Madison
MICHAEL P. DOYLE, Department of Food Science and Technology, University of Georgia
JOHANNA T. DWYER, Frances Stern Nutrition Center,
    New England Medical Center Hospital, Boston
JOHN W. ERDMAN, JR., University of Illinois, Urbana
CUTBERTO GARZA, Division of Nutritional Sciences, Cornell University
K. MICHAEL HAMBIDGE, Department of Pediatrics,
    University of Colorado Medical Center, Denver
JANET C. KING, Department of Nutritional Sciences,
    University of California, Berkeley
LAURENCE N. KOLONEL, Cancer Center of Hawaii, University of Hawaii, Honolulu
SANFORD MILLER, Graduate School of Biomedical Sciences, University of Texas,
    San Antonio
ALFRED SOMMER,* School of Hygiene and Public Health, The Johns Hopkins University
VERNON R. YOUNG,* Laboratory of Human Nutrition,
    Massachusetts Institute of Technology
STEVE L. TAYLOR (*Ex Officio*), Department of Food Science and Technology,
    University of Nebraska
ARTHUR H. RUBENSTEIN* (*IOM Council Liaison*), Department of Medicine,
    The University of Chicago

Staff

CATHERINE E. WOTEKI, Director
MARCIA LEWIS, Administrative Assistant
SUSAN WYATT, Financial Associate

* Member, Institute of Medicine
† Member, National Academy of Sciences

BOARD ON HEALTH SCIENCES POLICY

J. CLAUDE BENNETT* (*Chair*), Department of Medicine, The University of Alabama
    School of Medicine, Birmingham
DAVID R. CHALLONER,* University of Florida
RAMZI S. COTRAN,* Harvard Medical School, Department of Pathology
DEBORAH COTTON,* Health Policy & Management, Harvard School of Public Health
EMILIO DADDARIO,* Attorney, Washington, D.C.
WILLIAM N. HUBBARD, JR.,* Retired President, The Upjohn Company,
    Hickory Corners, Michigan
THOMAS INUI,* Department of Ambulatory Care and Prevention,
    Harvard Medical School
RICHARD J. JOHNS,* Department of Biomedical Engineering,
    The Johns Hopkins University School of Medicine
ERIC R. KANDEL,* Center for Neurobiology & Behavior,
    Columbia College of Physicians and Surgeons
PATRICIA A. KING,* Georgetown University Law Center
ELAINE L. LARSON, School of Nursing, Georgetown University
JOSHUA LEDERBERG,* The Rockefeller University
ROBERT I. LEVY,* Wyeth-Ayerst Research, Philadelphia
MARY LAKE POLAN, Department of Obstetrics and Gynecology, Stanford University
JOHN D. STOBO, Department of Medicine and Physician-In-Chief,
    The Johns Hopkins Hospital
JOHN E. WENNBERG,* The Center for the Evaluative Clinical Sciences,
    Dartmouth Medical School
JEAN DONALD WILSON, Department of Internal Medicine, University of Texas,
    Southwestern Medical Center, Dallas

Staff

VALERIE P. SETLOW, Director
RUTH E. BULGER, Senior Program Officer
JOSEPH CASSELLS, Senior Program Officer
PHILOMINA MAMMEN, Administrative Assistant

*Member, Institute of Medicine

Preface

For many years women have not been included in large prospective trials examining the benefits and risks of therapeutic interventions in diseases with significant morbidity and mortality that are common to both men and women. Such exclusion was not due to a lack of concern for the health of women, but rather an assumption that results obtained in men could be extrapolated to women. Other reasons for excluding women from clinical trials included concerns about the difficulty of recruiting and retaining women as compared with men and the need to increase sample size and costs. Implicit in the argument for larger sample sizes, ironically, is the need for a separate analysis by gender, which undercuts the assumption that the results can be extrapolated from males to females.

More recent research with drug therapy has shown important pharmacokinetic differences between males and females, as well as differences in risks and, in some cases, benefits. Thus, it is appropriate to conduct large scale studies in women who have or acquire diseases that are common to both sexes. In addition, women are at great risk for diseases like osteoporosis and breast cancer, for which additional prevention strategies are sorely needed.

The National Institutes of Health (NIH) has invested considerable resources in the past few years to rectify the inequities in research involving women and much useful information is expected to accrue from these efforts. The Women's Health Initiative (WHI) goes beyond NIH's earlier efforts—it is an attempt to not only gather data from over 100,000 women, but also to influence a change in lifestyles toward a healthier future.

The committee constituted by the Institute of Medicine (IOM) to review the WHI protocol faced a challenging task of reviewing a study that already had awarded large multi-year contracts and that was to begin participant recruitment during the IOM committee's review period.

There is a tension evident throughout this report. Had this committee been asked to design a plan for women's health research, it would not have designed this WHI. Although some committee members would have preferred that the WHI be cancelled, others were more willing to take the gamble. The committee focused on what aspects of the WHI it did and did not consider scientifically justifiable and feasible. As will be seen, the committee recommended that the ongoing WHI could proceed but should be modified.

The committee wishes to express its appreciation to the many people who made important contributions to this report by providing source materials or special written reports, sharing their views during meetings, commenting on drafts, or otherwise serving as resource persons. In particular, the committee wishes to thank Dr. Louise Brinton, National Cancer Institute; Dr. M.R.C. Greenwood, University of California at Davis; Dr. J. Christopher Gallagher, Creighton University Medical Center; Dr. David Hunter, Harvard University; Dr. William Insull, Lipid Research Clinic, Houston, TX; Gayle Mowbray, The Johns Hopkins University; Paul Phelps, a free-lance editor and writer; Dr. John Potter, University of Minnesota; and Dr. Christopher Sempos, National Center for Health Statistics.

Many people at NIH shared generously of their time to supply the committee with the documents necessary to perform this review. Susan Clark, Project Officer; Dr. Caroline Clifford, Chief, Diet and Cancer Branch, National Cancer Institute; Laurence Freedman, Acting Chief, Biometry Branch, NCI; Linda Gardner, Contracts Specialist; Dr. William Harlan, Co-Director, WHI; Dr. Carrie Hunter, Special Assistant to the Director, Office of Research on Women's Health; and Dr. Jacques Rossouw, Project Officer, WHI Clinical Trial and Observational Study went to special efforts to assist IOM staff.

The committee would also like to thank Dr. Ross Prentice, Principal Investigator of the WHI Clinical Coordinating Center, and the representatives from the Vanguard Clinical Centers, who were able to join the committee on extremely short notice for its July 1993 meeting and provided valuable information about details of the WHI.

The necessity for rapid review required herculean efforts on the part of the IOM staff, particularly the Study Director, Dr. Susan Thaul, to prepare background material and to formulate the issues for review. The committee itself had only three meetings, at monthly intervals, to debate the issues and to prepare draft statements on several topics. At these meetings, and also behind the scenes, Dr. Thaul and Dr. Catherine E. Woteki, the Director of the IOM's Food and Nutrition Board, provided skillful guidance and input.

The study report itself was thoroughly prepared by Dr. Thaul and Dana Hotra, Research Associate. They not only had to synthesize the discussions that took place at the meetings but also to interpret a multiplicity of comments and recommendations into a report with which all members could agree. In addition, they made major contributions to the report using their own expertise. The committee could not have accomplished its goals in the brief period allotted to it without their dedicated efforts.

The committee also wishes to thank Dr. Ruth Bulger, the past Director of the IOM Health Sciences Policy Division, who was instrumental in developing this project for the IOM; Claudia Carl, Administrative Associate in the IOM Reports and Information Office; Robert Earl, Program Officer; Michael Edington, Managing Editor, Reports and Information

PREFACE

Office; Geraldine Kennedo, Project Assistant; Felice LePar, Research Assistant; Marcia Lewis, Administrative Assistant; Dr. Valerie P. Setlow, Director of the Health Sciences Policy Division of the IOM; Susan M. Wyatt, IOM Financial Associate; and the staff of the Food and Nutrition Board for their support.

Finally, much appreciation is also due to Donna Allen, Project Assistant, who smoothed the way for the committee members and the rest of the IOM staff.

Marion J. Finkel, M.D.
Chair

Contents

Executive Summary 1
    The Women's Health Initiative, 2
    The IOM Study, 3
    Findings and Suggestions, 4
      Clinical Trial, 4
      Observational Study, 9
      Community Prevention Study, 9
    Recommendations, 10
      Clinical Trial, 10
      Observational Study, 11
      Community Prevention Study, 12
    Responses to the Statement of Task, 13

1 Introduction 19
    Description of the NIH Women's Health Initiative, 20
    History of Institute of Medicine Involvement, 20
    Committee Selection and Participation, 21
    Statement of Task, 21
    Committee Activities, 23

2 Clinical Trial 25
    Introduction, 25
    Rationale, 26
      General Issues, 26
      Integration of the CT with Other Components of the WHI, 28
    Design and Methods, 29
      Factorial Design, 29
      Sample Characteristics, 30
      Proposed Analytic Techniques, 34
      Ethics: Consent and Stopping Rules, 35
      Minority Analysis Plan, 39

　　　　Specifying the Relationship of Intervention and Effect, 40
　　　　Outcome Definition and Measurement, 40
　　　　Recruitment and Retention, 41
　　　　Adherence, 44
　　　　Secular Trends, 45
　　　　Provision of Health Care Services to Participants, 45
　　　　Study Management, 46
　　　Dietary Modification Branch, 47
　　　　Rationale, 47
　　　　Design and Methods, 49
　　　　Weighing Benefits and Uncertainties of the Breast
　　　　　Cancer Arm, 51
　　　Hormone Replacement Therapy Branch, 52
　　　　Rationale, 52
　　　　Design and Methods, 53
　　　　Threats to Completion of HRT Branch, 54
　　　　Use of HRT in Elderly Women, 56
　　　Calcium and Vitamin D Supplement Branch, 59
　　　　Rationale, 59
　　　　Design and Methods, 60
　　　　Threats to Successful Completion of CaD Branch, 61
　　　Clinical Trial Cost, 61
　　　　Data Available to Committee Deliberations, 62
　　　　WHI Cost Relative to Other Large Studies, 63
　　　　Clinical Center Funding, 64
　　　　Total Cost, 65
　　　　Potential Causes of Budget Shortfalls, 66
　　　　Summary, 68
　　　Findings and Suggestions, 69
　　　Recommendations, 73

3　Observational Study 77
　　　Rationale, 77
　　　Design and Methods, 78
　　　Cost, 79
　　　Recommendations, 80

4 Community Prevention Study 81
   Introduction, 81
   Rationale, 81
   Design and Methods, 82
   Cost, 83
   Recommendations, 83

5 Concluding Remarks 85
   Response to the Statement of Task, 85
   Societal Context, 88
      Efficacy and Effectiveness, 88
      Public Health Choice Versus Individual Choice, 89
      Considerations Beyond Science, 90

References 91

Appendix A Clinical Trial Exclusion Criteria 97

Appendix B U.S. House of Representatives Appropriations
            Committee 101

Appendix C Statement of Task 103

Appendix D Documents Received by the Institute of Medicine from the
            National Institutes of Health 105

Appendix E Meeting Participants June, July, and August 1993 109

Appendix F Primary and Subsidiary Hypotheses of the Women's Health Initiative
            Clinical Trial 113

Appendix G Women's Health Initiative Committees 115

Appendix H NIH-Sponsored Women's Health Studies 117

Appendix I NIH Cost and FTE Summary for Vanguard Clinical Centers 123

Appendix J NIH Power Calculations 127

Appendix K Women's Health Initiative Clinical Coordinating Center and
            Vanguard Clinical Centers Principal Investigators 133

Appendix L Abbreviations and Acronyms 135

Appendix M Committee and Staff Biographies 137

List of Figures

1 Objective Prescheduled Reassessment (OPR) Time Frame, 17
2-1 Outcomes for WHI Clinical Trial, 27
2-2 Women's Health Initiative Clinical Trial Partial Factorial Design, 30
2-3 NIH Organization for the WHI, 47
2-4 Objective Prescheduled Reassessment Timeline, 76

Executive Summary

A growing recognition of the importance of research on women's health, sparked by concern for the treatment and prevention of breast cancer, has led the National Institutes of Health (NIH) to launch the Women's Health Initiative (WHI). This unprecedented study will involve approximately 160,000 women at 45 clinical centers and thousands of others in community studies over a period of 14 years. The WHI will investigate strategies for preventing three of the leading causes of death and decreased quality of life for older women—cardiovascular disease, breast cancer, and osteoporotic fractures. But while recruitment of study participants has already begun, serious questions remain about the design, timetable, and likely results of this $625 million public investment.

Biomedical research is always a gamble; no study can be guaranteed to find useful prevention or treatment strategies. Nor can one study answer all pertinent questions. But when NIH undertakes a research project as costly and complex as the WHI, one would like to increase the likelihood that the research will yield definitive answers to important health questions. Clear goals, wise planning, adequate funding, and sufficient flexibility to deal with the unknown—all will help to increase the chances of success.

As described in the report, the committee had a defined charge: to determine whether the WHI or parts of it could be justified scientifically. The committee's charge was *not* to design a women's health study as if the WHI did not exist, nor was its task to decide whether other designs were preferable.

The task of the committee was shaped by the fact that the committee was assessing a research project at the worst possible time. The project was already underway, but it was too early to have proof of adequate implementation or to have any findings. Public funds had already been committed to institutions and investigators, and public expectations had been raised. These considerations did have some influence on the recommendations made by the committee.

This report acknowledges the planning and preparation done by the scientists at NIH, the Vanguard Clinical Centers, and the WHI advisory committees. Following its review, the committee's overall recommendation is that the ongoing WHI study could proceed but it should be modified. In order to provide a basis for improvement, however, the report focuses on identifying potential problems and finding strategies for dealing with them, in order to increase the probability that the WHI will make a meaningful contribution to the health of women in the United States.

THE WOMEN'S HEALTH INITIATIVE

The WHI is the largest research study ever funded by NIH. Budgeted at $625 million over 14 years, it is designed to test strategies to prevent cardiovascular disease, breast cancer, and osteoporotic fractures—leading causes of death, disability, and decreased quality of life for older women.

The WHI consists of three major components: the Clinical Trial, the Observational Study, and the Community Prevention Study. By far the costliest and most complex of these components is the Clinical Trial (CT), which will involve 63,000 postmenopausal women at 45 clinical centers across the United States. The CT has three branches that, as currently designed, will test several hypotheses:

- **Dietary Modification (DM)**
  Primary hypotheses:
   A low fat dietary pattern reduces the risk of breast cancer and colorectal cancer.
  Secondary hypothesis:
   A low fat dietary pattern reduces the risk of coronary heart disease.

- **Hormone Replacement Therapy (HRT)**
  Primary hypothesis:
   Estrogen replacement therapy (ERT) and progestin and estrogen replacement therapy (PERT) reduce the risk of cardiovascular disease.
  Secondary hypotheses:
   ERT and PERT reduce the risk of osteoporotic fractures.
   ERT and PERT increase the risk of breast cancer.

- **Calcium and Vitamin D Supplementation (CaD)**
  Primary hypothesis:
   Supplementation reduces the risk of hip fractures.
  Secondary hypotheses:
   Supplementation reduces the risk of other fractures.
   Supplementation reduces the risk of colorectal cancer.

The Observational Study will interview, obtain blood specimen samples from, and follow another 100,000 women who were ineligible or unwilling to participate in the CT, generating a rich database on the CT hypotheses and related health questions. Committee calculations corroborated by estimates provided by the Clinical Coordinating Center, find the CT and the

OS together are budgeted at $586 million. The Community Prevention Study will involve thousands of other women in the development of community-based strategies and infrastructure to promote healthy behaviors and practices to decrease the risk of morbidity and mortality. The CPS is under design and therefore does not have an announced budget.

THE IOM STUDY

Concern over the size and complexity of the WHI, as well as rapidly escalating cost estimates, led the U.S. House of Representatives' Appropriations Committee to direct NIH to contract with the Institute of Medicine (IOM) for a review of the proposed Initiative. To respond to this request, the IOM constituted the Committee to Review the NIH Women's Health Initiative.

Under the terms of this request, the IOM review of the WHI has focused on four principal questions:

1. *Topics considered.* What was the rationale behind the choice of these particular studies? Are appropriate topics considered? Should other topics be included?

2. *Methodology.* Are the methodologies and the study designs appropriate to address the stated research objectives? Is the size of the study population appropriate?

3. *Costs.* Are the costs accurately estimated and sufficient to reach the desired objectives?

4. *Justification.* Will the study produce sufficiently reliable results to justify the costs?

Questions 3 and 4 paraphrase the language in the House Appropriations report: "This study should focus on the issue of cost, as well as the issue of whether the study will produce sufficiently reliable results to justify such a massive investment."[*] In order to answer question 4, however, it is necessary to answer question 3 first. Whatever the total cost, inadequate funding based on inaccurate estimates of staff, equipment, space, and time would severely threaten the completion of the project. At the opposite end of a cost estimate error, overfunding would not be an appropriate use of scarce public funds.

Cost estimates could be exquisitely accurate yet not be justified by the results if the structure of the study design were flawed to the extent that it could not answer the study questions. Hence, the IOM committee considered it within its charge to address question 2—to review the study design and statistical methods proposed by NIH.

---

[*] U.S. House of Representatives, Departments of Labor, Health and Human Services, and Education, and Related Agencies Appropriations Bill, 1993, Report 102-809, p. 90.

Finally, of what use is a well-designed, well-funded study, if the questions it asks are ill-conceived? To answer the bottom-line question 4, the committee needed first to discuss the rationale of the WHI and its component parts, that is, question 1.

It was *not* the committee's task to design a women's health study as if the WHI did not exist. In fact, the committee expressed concern that a precedent not be set whereby Congress exercised oversight with respect to research designs or mandated special review committees for all large trials after the normal review processes have taken place. The committee was charged to begin with the WHI design, to consider threats to its successful completion—whether methodological, financial, or ethical—and to consider whether it would yield reliable results. After consultation with IOM and Congressional staff, the committee chose in this context to interpret "reliable" to denote "meaningful" rather than, in the statistical sense, "repeatable." This was the intent of the Appropriations Committee in raising the question.

FINDINGS AND SUGGESTIONS

The committee feels that the WHI had inadequate peer review from within NIH or from outside scientists. Although various elements of the WHI were reviewed at one time or another (e.g., the dietary modification trial was reviewed multiple times in earlier proposals, none of which were allowed to proceed), the committee's impression is that the complicated interlocking combination of the clinical trial and the observational study was not reviewed as rigorously as the usual Institute-initiated project. It seems that this inter-Institute study fell outside the review process.

> • *The committee suggests that NIH reexamine and strengthen the mechanism through which it reviews future inter-Institute proposed projects.*

Clinical Trial

The committee concentrated on two fundamental questions:

Can the design answer the questions it addresses, if no operational difficulties occur?

If the study design is appropriate, what threats are there to the successful completion of the study?

The committee identified seven issues involving conceptual problems that are built into the design. Even if all study operations were to proceed without incident, these design issues threaten the validity of the findings. Where appropriate, the committee has also suggested strategies to overcome the difficulties.

Factorial Design

NIH argued that conducting a partial factorial design would reduce the required number of women and attendant costs and allow assessment of interactions among intervention branches. The committee feels that the factorial design has major drawbacks. The overlap of 15.9 percent between the DM and HRT interventions is insufficient to provide adequate statistical power to assess interactions, and the difficulties of maintaining adherence to two or three interventions detracts from the attractiveness of a factorial design. In essence, the integrated design has become primarily a matter of economic efficiency; it is not essential to hypothesis testing.

Sample Characteristics

In determining sample size, the study design relies heavily on extremely uncertain assumptions regarding magnitude of effect and lag times. This concern is a factor in the recommendation described below regarding study duration.

Participants will not be categorized by risk for breast cancer, colorectal cancer, or coronary heart disease. This allows a more generalizable study, but the lack of risk restrictions requires a much larger sample size. The factorial design does not allow specific branches to focus on the most efficient samples, such as women at high risk of CHD for an HRT trial or women at high risk of breast cancer for a DM trial, according to NIH assumptions.

Proposed Analytic Techniques

Committee concerns center on choice of endpoints for trial closeout and the planned use of methods to adjust for multiple comparisons when considering interim decisions by the Data and Safety Monitoring Board (DSMB).

- *The committee suggested that unadjusted data be made available to the DSMB. The committee felt that the Bonferroni statistical adjustment, for which current analysis plans call, might be too conservative and therefore might deprive many participants of an appropriately timed conclusion to the study.*

- *The committee also suggested the use of a two-sided test of significance to maintain a scientifically-justified neutral stance regarding whether the interventions might yield beneficial or adverse effects.*

Ethics

The informed consent measures do not provide an adequate understanding of the likelihood or magnitude of major risks and benefits. The obligation to inform potential and current research participants would require much more information at the outset, as well as a commitment to provide evolving information over the course of the project.

> *• The committee believes that studywide material must inform potential participants of risks as well as benefits. The committee suggested that the counselors at the clinical centers be knowledgeable and have access to algorithms, guidelines, and printed material about known risks and benefits. These counselors would need supervision, training, and monitoring. In addition, new information from this as well as other pertinent trials (as judged by the WHI coordinators and the DSMB) must be shared with the participants to allow them to make their own decisions about ongoing risks and benefits of the interventions.*

The inclusion of several interventions with several endpoints in a single trial makes the stopping rules difficult to formulate.

> *• Therefore, the committee suggested that the DSMB should (a) use preexisting or external information to establish a prior probability that internal data could confirm (this might mean accepting an earlier "stopping" conclusion than would be justified by data arising solely from the CT); (b) perform pre-specified subset analyses on participants groups that are especially likely to evidence harm or benefit; (c) ask to examine uncorrected estimates of effect and do any analyses it feels are warranted; (4) review the monitoring of the consent process; and (5) evaluate pre-specified event rates for potential morbidity and mortality outcomes.*

Minority Analysis Plan

As currently designed, the study will have insufficient power to compare individual minority groups to the majority population. The study will be able to observe differences, if they exist, but will not be able to test them with adequate power.

> *• The committee encourages NIH to make these limitations known to those who may be expecting definitive comparative findings among minority and majority groups.*

Specificity of Intervention and Effect

The CT design does not distinguish which element of the low fat dietary pattern may be responsible for any observed outcome. Similarly, the design will not allow analyses to distinguish whether calcium or calcium plus vitamin D is responsible for any observed outcome. Because some endpoints can be affected by more than one of the study interventions, and because the factorial design is modified by participant decisions, the overlap and interactions will be difficult to analyze.

Outcome Definition and Measurement

Threats to accurate and unbiased endpoint detection include the obscure meaning of many mammography-detected tiny malignancies; the unstandardized method of detecting colorectal cancer; and the inadequate development of behavioral, psychological, and quality of life measures for use in the study.

- *The committee encourages NIH to include measures of constructs such as pain, mobility, and psychological status.*

In addition to the conceptual problems described above, any study—no matter how well designed—is subject to setbacks by operational problems. The WHI CT is particularly vulnerable to such problems because of its size, complexity, and duration. The committee has identified five operational issues that could jeopardize the success of the study:

Recruitment, Retention, and Adherence

The message of the study is not adequately developed and may be misleading.

- *The committee suggests that NIH and the clinical centers develop an overall message for the study that pays particular attention to long-term recruitment strategies for older and minority participants, and does not emphasize the WHI as a breast cancer prevention trial. In addition, investigators should set higher standards for studywide materials than currently appear to exist, including introductory brochures, consent forms, and videotape information. This information should be available in conversational language.*

NIH has made overly optimistic assumptions about recruitment, retention, and adherence, especially in subgroups with which researchers have less clinical trial experience, such as older women, minority women, and the spectrum of socioeconomic status (SES), and in recruitment plans that cover many years.

- *Nevertheless, the committee encourages NIH to seek diversity within the sample and suggests that attempts should be made to include the entire SES range in this study.*

The acceptability of the various branches of the CT to women is unclear at this stage, especially since the interventions are difficult and have potential side effects.

- *To maintain adequate statistical power, the CT must have funds available to boost recruitment efforts if, as the committee expects, recruitment rates are lower than anticipated.*

Secular Trends

If secular trends toward a decreasing fat content in the U.S. diet continue, and if there is appreciable nonadherence in the DM treatment group, the difference between the treatment and control diets is likely to be too small to show a treatment effect.

Provision of Health Care Services to Participants

The current protocol includes a referral to a regular source of care. This is not adequately responsible.

- *The committee suggests that the clinical centers must develop adequate links with reliable community providers to ensure that adequate follow-up care is available. It may become essential for the project to pay for some kinds of follow-up for some poor or uninsured women.*

Research staff need to spend considerable time discussing side effects with participants, and dealing with associated apprehension, both in the clinic and on the telephone. To fail to do so is to risk unethical behavior and increased study dropout. The current budget may not include adequate staff time for these activities.

Cost

The committee believes that the total costs of the CT will be greater than the $625 million provided by NIH. NIH and Vanguard Clinical Center representatives have indicated that the additional funds necessary for successful completion of the trial will be covered by the institutions in which the Clinical Centers are based. This reliance on institutional support may be reasonable in the case of the Vanguard Clinical Centers, but the committee felt it is unlikely that an additional 29 institutions can be identified that have both the experience to carry out the tasks of high quality research and the ability to provide additional resources.

Potential sources of budget shortfall include lagging participant recruitment, which could require increased staff resources; staff turnover, which could require training and travel resources and might delay recruitment, threaten adherence, and, therefore, affect study validity; and cross-over of participants between study intervention regimens and control status.

The CT funding per-person per-year is less than half that for other recent NIH studies of women's health, including, specifically, those that use similar drug regimens and approaches.

There does not seem to be a budget adjustment plan for unanticipated changes in either the scope of work or medical technology during the course of the trial.

- *In addition to its concerns about initial funding levels, the committee was concerned about long-term funding and suggested that NIH clarify what the contract requires financially in terms of anticipated or unanticipated changes throughout the duration of the study.*

Observational Study

Although NIH considers the Observational Study (OS) an important component of the WHI, the OS has not received the same amount of attention as has the CT. It is anticipated that the 45 clinical centers involved with the CT will enroll approximately 100,000 women, collecting baseline data and following them for an average of nine years. An observational study of this scope would require a very large investment if it were initiated independently, but since the OS was designed as a WHI component, the marginal cost of its addition is reasonable—as estimated at $105 per woman over the duration of the study by the Clinical Coordinating Center—in terms of the information it can acquire.

Community Prevention Study

NIH has not provided a clear vision for the Community Prevention Study (CPS). Because only an initial plan for the CPS has been presented thus far—with rationale, design and methods, and cost incompletely conceptualized—the committee was unsure of the scope of the CPS and the resources necessary to complete it.

Based on information available about the anticipated costs of the CT and OS, the committee calculates that as little as $25 million could be available for the CPS component of the WHI. Given the tremendous need for strategies that would result in lifestyle change in women, particularly among lower socioeconomic status and minority women, the committee feels strongly that the amount will not suffice.

The committee suggested that the following issues be highlighted in the development of the CPS protocol:

- *project selection should ensure that components are suitable for incorporation into comprehensive community-based programs;*
- *projects should attempt to decrease unfavorable disparities between lower SES and racial/ethnic minority women and higher SES nonminority women and to promote the creation of culturally appropriate strategies at low cost;*
- *projects should include strong training components (that will permit personnel to train others in additional communities), possibly resulting in a set of regional training centers;*
- *projects should employ many process measures needed for cost-effectiveness analyses; and*

- *NIH should favor projects that are multifactor in both risk factors and targeted methods of intervention.*

RECOMMENDATIONS

Clinical Trial

The committee was charged to begin with the existing WHI design, consider threats to its successful completion—whether design, financial, or ethical—and to consider whether it would yield reliable results.

- **The committee recommends that the dietary modification-breast cancer hypothesis be considered a subsidiary rather than a primary hypothesis, shifting the emphasis to the effect of dietary modification on coronary heart disease outcomes, making those the primary hypotheses.**

- **The committee recommends that the consent process be outlined more carefully, be conscientiously implemented and monitored across all centers, and be evaluated and updated as needed.**

- **The committee recommends that the CT be scheduled to end in mid-2002, rather than close out the interventions by April 2005, and that the findings of an Objective Prescheduled Reassessment (OPR) be available by April 2002 (see figure at the end of the Executive Summary).**

The OPR, managed through an internal or external review board, would consider whether continuation or modification of the CT could be justified. Recruitment for the CT began in September 1993, so the project would run unimpeded for more than eight years (unless the Data Safety and Monitoring Board moves to stop the trial sooner based on interim data). Data analysis would begin in October 2001 and conclude with a recommendation by April 2002. Between October 2001 and the decision to extend, modify, or terminate, the CT would continue in its active mode. Sufficient time would be provided for closeout or redesign and data analyses.

This recommendation addresses the primary concerns of the committee in the following ways:

- Data from nearly six years mean follow-up time would be available for the OPR. According to NIH power calculations, this timeframe would allow hypotheses regarding stronger, expected associations (HRT and coronary heart disease; and HRT and combined fractures) to be tested and findings disseminated in a timely manner. If the intervention effect is strong, this timeframe also allows the hypotheses regarding the weaker, expected associations (DM and coronary heart disease; CaD and hip fractures; and HRT and hip fractures) to be tested. This timeframe does not allow for adequate follow-up for the DM and breast cancer hypothesis, the DM and colorectal cancer hypothesis, or the HRT and breast cancer hypothesis. However, the committee feels that, as currently designed, the CT does not have a high probability of yielding statistically significant results for the DM and breast cancer hypothesis or the HRT and breast cancer hypothesis, even after more prolonged follow-up. The committee would therefore prefer to see the other hypotheses analyzed in an appropriate timeframe. While the DM and colorectal cancer hypothesis is strong, it alone does not justify continuing the CT.

- This recommendation allows an assessment that would be informed by recruitment, retention, adherence, and incidence experience; if any of these estimates have not been or are not being met, the problem can be addressed. For example, if HRT is demonstrated to be favorable compared with control, the CT could reassign the control participants (with their permission) to ERT or PERT, thus increasing statistical power for that direct comparison, which as designed is not currently adequate. If recruitment or adherence experience is so poor that an adequate test of a hypothesis would not be possible in any reasonable time frame, the CT or a branch of it could terminate. If, on the other hand, recruitment or adherence problems are discretely identifiable, the study could be redesigned for the remaining duration to compensate for these problems.

- Any clinically beneficial findings of the CT can be made available to participants. Clinical knowledge resulting from other studies can also be applied to participants in both intervention and control arms of the CT. Therefore, WHI investigators would not be pressured to deny benefits to women in the CT to keep intact its overlapping studies.

Observational Study

- **The committee recommends that NIH treat the OS as a precious investment even though its marginal cost to the WHI is low. The progress of the OS should be monitored carefully to ensure that the quality of the data is as high as possible, and that losses to follow-up are minimized.**

- **The committee recommends that NIH make OS data available to qualified investigators outside the WHI network early enough to maximize the use of the data. Outside investigators should also be able to add ancillary studies to the OS. Such data availability increases the scientific and public health yield of a public investment and would increase the justification of the expenditure. Clear policies about the timing and conditions under which the data and cohort will be made available to outside investigators need to be established from the outset.**

- The committee encourages both NIH and the WHI OS Subcommittee to consider the implications for the OS of the recommendation that the CT undergo an OPR after eight years. It is likely that contingency plans for the OS will need to be devised.

Community Prevention Study

- **The development of the Community Prevention Study is of equal importance to the CT and the OS. It urgently needs a more definitive plan and the committee recommends that NIH develop one quickly.**

The level of resources allocated for the CPS should be an affirmative decision, one that is based on the appropriate funding necessary to accomplish the task, not using only what funds might remain after the completion of the other two components of the WHI.

The committee also feels that certain aspects of the CPS are critical to highlight. While these are not as essential to WHI success as are the primary recommendations, the committee urges the NIH to seriously consider the following suggestions:

- Given the importance of women's health and the vast range of circumstances influencing it, numerous projects (probably between 40 and 50) should be funded over approximately eight years. These projects should adequately encompass needs related to diversity of health topic; intended recipients of interventions; geographic regions of varied cultures; and approach or strategy. Within the eight-year project, three years of funding is recommended in order to focus on strengthening infrastructure development and dissemination techniques.

- Approximately $50 to $100 million should be targeted for the CPS.

- Internal resources should be developed in conjunction with the coordinating and disseminating functions related to the CPS. In general, NIH should strengthen its public health and disease prevention component; the coordination and dissemination activities of the CPS can aid NIH in reaching that goal.

- NIH should ensure that a mechanism (such as comparable data collection instruments) exists to link the projects and facilitate useful exchanges among investigators. This would also serve to transfer knowledge and technology to relevant communities during a later dissemination phase. The cooperative agreement is considered as a possible mechanism for this purpose.

RESPONSES TO THE STATEMENT OF TASK

After reviewing the information provided by NIH and considering additional perspectives provided by the Vanguard Clinical Center* representatives and other researchers, the committee reached agreement about its responses to four questions posed in its statement of task. The responses are summarized in this Executive Summary and discussed more fully in the report.

1. What was the rationale behind the choice of these particular studies? Are appropriate topics considered? Should other topics be included?

NIH has provided a justifiable rationale for the diseases selected for study in the WHI. These diseases are important causes of morbidity and mortality among women in the United States; they merit further research to test the efficacy of preventive measures and to develop effective programs that educate and motivate women to adopt proven prevention strategies. Heart disease and cancer are the leading causes of death among women, and the high incidence of breast cancer is appropriately a matter of concern. Osteoporotic fractures, which occur with much higher frequency among women than men, are a leading cause of disability among older women. Research leading to prevention of these conditions, or at least postponement of the age of onset, would be expected to improve substantially the quality of life of older women.

NIH could have chosen other diseases or risk factors for ill health as the focus for the WHI, and those choices could also be defended. There are many unanswered questions regarding prevention of illness, enhancement of well-being, and delay of morbidity and mortality while maintaining an acceptable quality of life.

Because the WHI is among the most complex studies ever undertaken, and because the WHI Clinical Trial is already under way, it would not be appropriate to suggest other topics to be included. This might overburden an already complex set of studies, could incur additional costs, and would almost certainly lead to further delays. Moreover, as noted above, it was not the committee's task to redesign the WHI.

2. Are the methodologies and the study designs appropriate to address the stated research objectives? Is the size of the study population appropriate?

The methodologies selected—a clinical trial, an observational study, and community studies—are appropriate for the study of the efficacy or effectiveness of certain interventions to improve women's health, for generating further hypotheses, and for implementing and evaluating community intervention strategies. Because details of the CPS have not been

---

*The Vanguard Clinical Centers are the 16 clinical centers chosen by NIH to initiate the trial. An additional 29 clinical centers are scheduled to begin in 1994.

decided, little can be said about the appropriateness of the specific methods and designs of the study. The majority of NIH staff time and effort has been devoted to designing the CT; therefore, it is the focus of most of the comments and recommendations in this report.

Three primary hypotheses are the basis of the CT:

- A low fat dietary pattern will reduce the incidence of breast cancer and colorectal cancer;
- Hormone replacement therapy will reduce the incidence of cardiovascular disease; and
- Calcium and vitamin D supplements will reduce the incidence of osteoporotic hip fracture.

The design of the trial, the number of women who will participate, and the methods used to determine health status all flow from these hypotheses. Some of the design decisions are based on evidence obtained from earlier studies, and some decisions are based on assumptions. Assumptions must be made regarding many aspects of any clinical trial, and examples include the strength of the protective effect, the number and timing of the endpoint events (occurrence of heart attacks, hip fractures, breast cancer), the ability to recruit and retain the study participants, and the ability to maintain adherence and behavior change in the intervention groups.

To determine whether the proposed methods for the CT were appropriate for the stated research objectives, the committee analyzed the assumptions underlying the methods for each hypothesis and identified the major threats to the successful achievement of each hypothesis. The committee then weighed the risks of an unsuccessful trial against the potential benefits of additional information to be learned from a successful trial.

Using this approach, the primary hypothesis that a low fat dietary pattern will reduce breast cancer and colorectal cancer incidence was judged by the committee to be inappropriate for emphasis as a primary hypothesis in the trial. The primary hypotheses of the HRT branch and the CaD branches were judged to be appropriate.

Several secondary hypotheses are also included in the design of the CT. Most prominent is the hypothesis that a low fat dietary pattern will reduce the incidence of cardiovascular disease. Using the same approach weighing the threats of an unsuccessful trial against the benefits of a successful trial, the committee judged this secondary hypothesis to be appropriate for inclusion in the trial.

These conclusions led to the specific recommendations about the design and conduct of the CT which have been presented.

3. Are the costs accurately estimated and sufficient to reach the desired objectives?

Cost estimates are fairly well developed for the CT, deducible for the OS, and absent for the CPS. To a large extent, this reflects the stage of development of each component. It is therefore difficult to say with certainty that overall costs are sufficient to reach the objectives of the WHI.

The CT appears to be very tightly budgeted. Although the approximately $1000 per-participant per-year costs are within the range of costs (unadjusted for inflation) NIH incurred for other clinical trials conducted over the past 20 years, they are very low relative to the costs of more recently conducted comparable trials.

As noted earlier in the Executive Summary, the committee believes that the total costs of the CT will be greater than the $625 million provided by NIH. NIH and Vanguard Clinical Center representatives have indicated that the additional funds necessary for successful completion of the trial will be covered by the institutions in which the Vanguard Clinical Centers are based. This reliance on institutional support may be reasonable in the case of the Vanguard Clinical Centers, but the committee felt it is unlikely that an additional 29 institutions can be identified that have both the experience to carry out the tasks of high quality research and the ability to provide additional resources. If all participating institutions honor their agreements to provide additional support for the CT, and if there are no unanticipated problems, the budgeted amount might be sufficient. However, it is very unlikely that there will be no problems.

4. Will the study produce sufficiently reliable results to justify the costs?

The committee concluded that valuable scientific information could be obtained in the redesigned study. However, the question of whether the investment is justified is, in part, a question about cost-effectiveness, and that involves consideration of alternative study designs. The committee thought it likely that much of the information could be obtained in better designed, smaller, more focused studies that could have a greater chance of success and probably be less costly. It recognized however, that a study in a broad-based population can have merit and proponents as well. The committee did not consider its task to be the consideration of alternative designs, and therefore did not do so. Thus, the committee admits some skepticism about the merits of this particular investment, but it cannot offer a definitive conclusion about cost-effectiveness.

It is important to note that the modified study that the committee felt could be justified scientifically is quite different in its aims from the study proposed by NIH. The study proposed by NIH has as a primary focus the test of whether DM will reduce the risk of breast cancer. The modified study focuses on coronary heart disease. If NIH decides to accept the recommendations of the committee about modification of the study, it will need to consider whether the methods and study population proposed to test interventions on the risk of both coronary heart disease and breast cancer should be the same as those for a test of effects on the risk of coronary heart disease. Moreover, NIH will need to consider whether the study objectives that can be achieved in the modified study are worth the investment.

Whatever the merits of the WHI, the committee has no doubt about the need for a substantial investment in research on women's health.

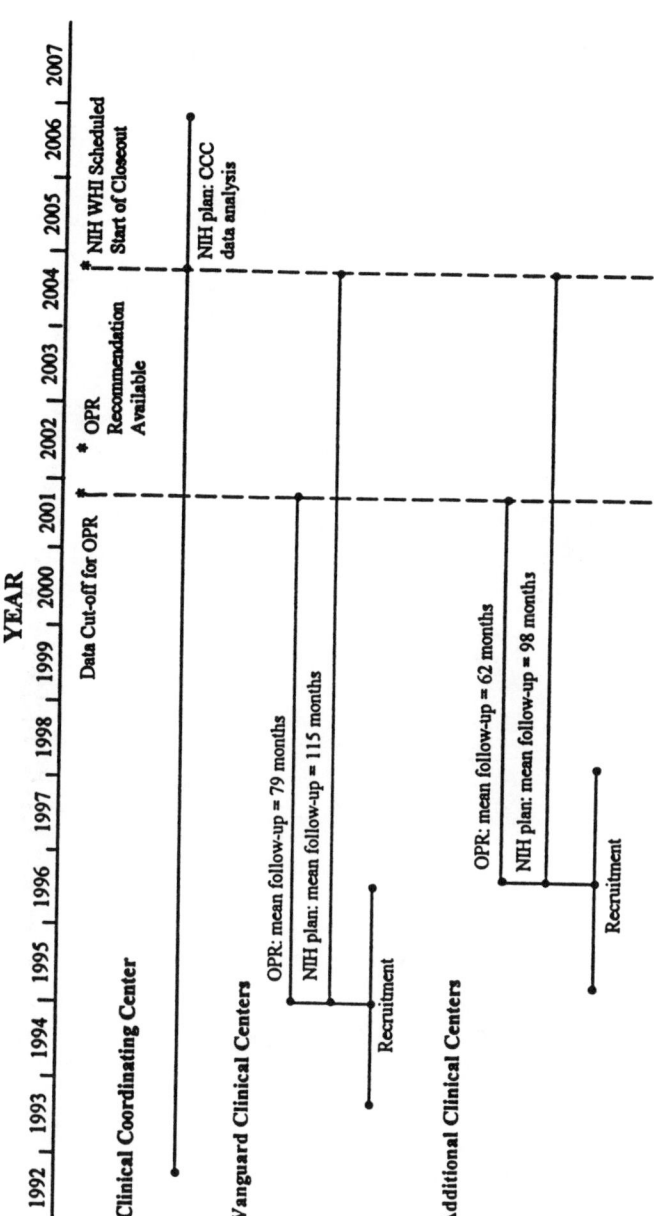

Figure 1   Objective Prescheduled Reassessment (OPR) time frame.

1

Introduction

Has research into women's health come into its own? The growing recognition of its importance by the Executive Branch of the government, the first female director of the National Institutes of Health (NIH), the consumer lobbies for treatment and prevention of breast cancer, the Congressional Caucus on Women's Issues, and hard-working researchers has culminated in the Women's Health Initiative. This 14-year, three-component project, budgeted at $625 million, is the largest single research study to be funded by NIH. As planned, it would involve 160,000 postmenopausal women at 45 clinical centers across the country and many other women residing in the communities that would participate in the Community Prevention Study.

The NIH Women's Health Initiative (WHI) is designed to learn about strategies to prevent breast cancer, cardiovascular disease, and osteoporotic fractures—leading causes of death and decreased quality of life for older women. Were the $625 million public investment guaranteed to find useful prevention or treatment strategies, it is hard to imagine many objections to the expenditure. Research is always a gamble, however. Simply put, if one knew the answer, one would not need to do the research. When NIH undertakes a research project that is as costly and complex as the WHI, it is necessary to maximize the likelihood that the research will yield definitive answers to important health questions. Clear goals, wise reasoning and planning, and funding adequate to the task are all essential to increasing the chances of success.

Scientists at NIH, the Vanguard Clinical Centers of the WHI, and advisory committees have contributed wisdom, time, and experience to building the WHI. Nagging doubt exists, however, that political concerns influenced the design, timetable, and budget of the study. The task of this committee is to respond to the concerns of the Committee on Appropriations of the U.S. House of Representatives over the study's design, its concomitant cost, and the probability that the WHI will produce results that will be meaningful to the health of women in the United States. The committee's goal was to evaluate whether the investment in the WHI can be expected to produce useful enough results to justify the cost.

DESCRIPTION OF THE NIH WOMEN'S HEALTH INITIATIVE

The WHI is an NIH-developed and funded study focusing on the health of postmenopausal women in the United States. Its three components are the Clinical Trial, the Observational Study, and the Community Prevention Study. NIH plans to administer the WHI, budgeted at $625 million over 14 years of activities, as two separate parts. A contract mechanism is in place for the Clinical Trial and Observational Study: a Clinical Coordinating Center and 16 Vanguard Clinical Centers began recruitment on September 1, 1993; in July 1993 NIH issued a Request for Proposals for an additional 29 Clinical Centers. The Community Prevention Study, which the NIH anticipates funding through Requests for Applications under a cooperative agreement, will be administered separately.

The Clinical Trial (CT), designed to include approximately 63,000 women, has three major branches, each based on a hypothesized intervention to prevent morbidity and mortality. Appendix A describes exclusion criteria. The diet modification branch, the primary endpoints of which are breast and colorectal cancer, includes randomization either to a control group or to a group receiving instruction, guidance, and support of a low fat dietary pattern. The hormone replacement therapy branch will focus primarily on potential protection against cardiovascular disease as well as potential adverse effects on breast and endometrial cancer risks; participants will be randomized to estrogen alone, estrogen plus progestin, or placebo. In the calcium and vitamin D branch, the primary endpoint is osteoporotic hip fracture, and women will be randomized to supplementation or placebo. The CT is designed as a partial factorial study (Figure 2-2) in order to reduce participant recruitment and follow-up costs.

The Observational Study (OS) will use, and go beyond, questionnaire and examination data gathered in the recruitment and enrollment of women into the CT. Approximately 100,000 women, ineligible or unwilling to participate in the CT, are expected to participate in the OS. Information from baseline examinations and interviews, annual questionnaire follow-up, three-year clinic visit follow-up, and selected clinic follow-ups at three-year intervals thereafter, are expected to yield valuable data for generating and testing hypotheses and examining associations.

Details of the Community Prevention Study (CPS) have not yet been established by NIH. Its overall goal would be to develop and test various strategies to influence women to change health behaviors and practices in order to decrease the risk of morbidity and mortality.

HISTORY OF INSTITUTE OF MEDICINE INVOLVEMENT

Dr. Bernadine Healy, as NIH director-designate, announced at her 1991 Senate confirmation hearing that NIH would launch a massive research initiative in women's health—afield that had been inadequately funded and championed. In that public statement,

INTRODUCTION

Dr. Healy estimated a package that would cost approximately half a billion dollars. Soon afterwards, the estimate was adjusted to about $600 million.

The U.S. House of Representatives' Appropriations Committee—one of the purposes of which includes attention to the uses of the public's money—was concerned that the rapid escalation in cost estimates might be a signal of poor planning. In its July 23, 1992, report (Appendix B), the Appropriations Committee directed NIH to contract with the Institute of Medicine (IOM) to complete a review of the design and estimated costs of the WHI by February 1, 1993, in time to make adjustments, if necessary, before major study activities began. The House Appropriations Committee report (102-809:90) stated:

> the study design and cost estimates should be thoroughly reviewed by an external group with expertise in this area. . . . This study should focus on the issue of cost, as well as the issue of whether the study will produce sufficiently reliable results to justify such a massive investment.

NIH first formally approached IOM in February 1993 to discuss the Appropriations Committee-requested project. NIH signed a contract allowing IOM to hire staff and begin work on April 23, 1993, well after the due date of the study requested by the Congress. Whether the delay was due to a slow-moving bureaucracy or to other causes is unknown to the IOM committee. As a result, however, the committee was faced with the task of critiquing a study in progress. In the interim, NIH had requested, received, and evaluated proposals, and entered into contracts with 17 research institutions to serve as the Clinical Coordinating Center and Vanguard Clinical Centers. Those funded centers have drafted an operating manual, hired staff, publicized the WHI in their communities, and begun to recruit participants.

COMMITTEE SELECTION AND PARTICIPATION

IOM formed a committee with a neutral core, supplemented by additional members that included some members perceived to be in favor of and others opposed to basic elements in the WHI design. The chair was chosen to be both neutral and out of the arena in which WHI funds might be sought. Committee members represent expertise in the areas of epidemiology, clinical trial design and implementation, community trials, biostatistics, health education, ethics, nutrition, dietary assessment and dietary modification, hormone replacement therapy, cardiovascular disease, breast cancer, osteoporosis, and geriatrics.

STATEMENT OF TASK

The Statement of Task (Appendix C), approved by the IOM Governing Board and reflected in the contract with NIH, requested an examination of four issues:

1. *Rationale for topics*. What was the rationale behind the choice of these particular studies? Are appropriate topics considered? Should other topics be included?

2. *Methodology*. Are the methodologies and the study designs appropriate to address the stated research objectives? Is the size of the study population appropriate?

3. *Costs*. Are the costs accurately estimated and sufficient to reach the desired objectives?

4. *Justification*. Will the study produce sufficiently reliable results to justify the costs?

Questions 3 and 4 paraphrase the language in the House Appropriations report: "This [IOM] study should focus on the issue of cost, as well as the issue of whether the study will produce sufficiently reliable results to justify such a massive investment."

In order to answer question 4, however, it is necessary to first answer question 3. Whatever the total cost, inadequate funding based on inaccurate estimates of staff, equipment, space, and time would severely threaten the completion of the project. At the opposite extreme, overfunding would not be an appropriate use of scarce public funds.

Cost estimates could be exquisitely accurate, yet not be justified by the results if the study design were flawed to the extent that it did not provide a structure by means of which the study questions could be answered. Hence, the IOM committee considered it within its charge to address question 2—to review the study design and statistical methods proposed by NIH.

Finally, of what use is a well-designed, well-funded study, if the questions it asks are not well conceived? In order to answer the bottom line question 4, the IOM committee needed also to discuss the rationale of the WHI and its component parts—that is, question 1.

It was *not* the committee's task to design a women's health study as if the WHI did not exist, nor was its task to decide whether other designs were preferable. In fact, the committee expressed concern that a precedent not be set whereby Congress exercised oversight with respect to research designs. The committee was charged to begin with the existing WHI design, consider threats to its successful completion—whether design, financial, or ethical—and to consider whether it would yield reliable results. The committee chose in this context to interpret "reliable" to denote "meaningful" rather than, in the statistical sense, "repeatable." To be meaningful in terms of public health significance, findings must meet some standard of internal validity, precision, and external validity.

Politics—the expression of community standards and desires—has been present throughout the development of the WHI and its precursor designs. Questions of feasibility and worth require judgments that are informed by both scientific and community standards. The IOM review has focused on the science base in dealing with the selection of committee members, topics to review, and the content of the report.

INTRODUCTION

In writing the report, the committee agreed that it was not appropriate to include an extensive literature review of the interventions and diseases on which the WHI focuses. Although the committee reviewed the relevant literature and applied it when assessing the Initiative, this report is not intended to be a resource document for such literature.

COMMITTEE ACTIVITIES

An 11-member committee, as described above, held three meetings in Washington, D.C., in June, July, and August 1993. To assess whether the costs estimated are sufficient to carry out the planned design, the committee requested numerous documents from NIH, some under the Freedom of Information Act mechanism. The committee reviewed some available documents (Appendix D), and held extensive discussions with the NIH scientists (Appendix E) at its June meeting and in subsequent telephone and written contacts. At its July meeting, the committee met with representatives of the NIH-funded WHI Clinical Coordinating Center and 15 of the 16 Vanguard Clinical Centers (Appendix E). These contacts allowed the committee to garner not only the facts but a feel for the organization and philosophy of the WHI.

The following chapters present the committee's findings, questions, and recommendations with regard to the WHI Clinical Trial (Chapter 2), Observational Study (Chapter 3), and Community Prevention Study (Chapter 4). A final chapter presents the committee's response to the questions it was charged to answer, along with concluding remarks on the societal context of the WHI and of biomedical research in general.

2

Clinical Trial

INTRODUCTION

This chapter focuses on the Clinical Trial (CT), which is the costliest, most complicated, and most controversial component of the Women's Health Initiative (WHI). The CT is designed to test the benefits and risks of dietary modification (DM), hormone replacement therapy (HRT), and calcium and vitamin D supplements (CaD) on the health of postmenopausal women. The primary hypotheses of these three branches of the CT are: (1) whether a low fat dietary pattern reduces the risks of breast and colorectal cancers; (2) whether hormone replacement therapy reduces the risk of coronary heart disease (CHD); and (3) whether combined calcium and vitamin D supplementation reduces the risk of hip fractures.

NIH has structured the CT as a 3 x 2 x 2 partial factorial design involving 63,000 women between the ages of 50 and 79 (in addition, 100,000 women will be enrolled in the observational study). NIH has funded a Clinical Coordinating Center and the first 16 of 45 expected Clinical Centers. These 16 centers, called Vanguard Clinical Centers, began a three-year recruitment period on September 1, 1993. The additional clinical centers, to be named in September 1994, would begin recruitment in January 1995. Clinic closeout is scheduled to begin September 2004, followed by two years of data analysis by the Clinical Coordinating Center.

The CT is the most thoroughly designed aspect of the WHI thus far. The committee's assessment of it was therefore based on more information than was available for the Observational Study (Chapter 3) or the Community Prevention Study (Chapter 4); that is reflected in the size and scope of this chapter. The chapter begins with trial-wide issues of rationale and study design. This is followed by a presentation of more detailed information on each branch. Cost details for the entire CT are presented. The chapter concludes with a presentation of the committee's findings and suggestions, and major recommendations regarding the CT component of the WHI.

RATIONALE

General Issues

Cardiovascular disease, breast cancer, and osteoporotic fractures are among the leading causes of morbidity and mortality in postmenopausal women. As such, they are reasonable and defensible targets for a large prevention study. Coronary heart disease is the leading cause of death in U.S. women. The mortality and incidence rates of breast cancer are high; over an average 85-year lifespan, one in nine women develop breast cancer and approximately one in thirty die of it. Osteoporotic fractures, which are associated with aging, affect many more women than men; complications are life threatening and reduce both longevity and quality of life.

These diseases are not alone among the severe disablers of women, however. The CT does not directly address arthritis, dysmobility, poverty and isolation, depression, dementia, hearing, vision, and dental losses, and institutionalization. Neither does it address other compelling outcomes, such as dysfunction or pain, that are not linked to solitary etiologies. This should not imply that these issues are not troubling sources of morbidity, nor that they would be inappropriate targets for future prevention and treatment research. Similarly, that the focus of the CT is on postmenopausal women should not be mistaken for a disregard of the myriad unanswered questions about younger women, or about the effects of behavior and disease in earlier stages of life on morbidity and mortality in later stages. One study cannot answer all questions.

The primary hypotheses of the CT are as follows:

- A low fat dietary pattern reduces the risk of breast cancer.
- A low fat dietary pattern reduces the risk of colorectal cancer.
- Hormone replacement therapy reduces the risk of coronary heart disease.
- Calcium and vitamin D (combined) supplementation reduces the risk of hip fracture.

The numerous secondary hypotheses include: DM reduces risk of CHD; HRT increases risks of breast and endometrial cancers; HRT reduces risk of fractures; and CaD reduces risk of colorectal cancer. The CT outcomes are presented in Figure 2-1; the CT hypotheses are listed in Appendix F.

There are reasonably good rationales for some aspects of each of the three branches of the CT, although evidence for the central hypothesis for the DM branch—that a change to a low fat dietary pattern by women over the age of 50 will reduce the incidence of breast cancer over the following nine years—is the weakest and least consistent of the three. There are stronger rationales for expecting that there are effects of DM on colorectal cancer and various cardiovascular disease endpoints. Similarly, there is a strong rationale for the HRT branch, which will test not only the relationship between HRT and coronary heart disease,

Outcome	HRT	DM	CaD
CARDIOVASCULAR:			
Coronary heart disease	1°	2°	2°
Stroke	2°	2°	2°
Congestive heart failure	2°	2°	2°
Angina	2°	2°	2°
Peripheral vascular disease	2°	2°	2°
Coronary revascularization	2°	2°	2°
Total cardiovascular	2°	2°	2°
CANCER:			
Breast cancer	2°	1°	2°
Endometrial cancer	2°	2°	2°
Colorectal cancer		1°	2°
Ovarian cancer	2°	2°	
Total cancers	2°	2°	2°
FRACTURES:			
Hip	2°	2°	1°
Other Fractures	2°	2°	2°
Total fractures	2°	2°	2°
OTHER:			
Venous thromboembolic disease			
Pulmonary embolism	2°		
Deep vein thrombosis	2°		
Diabetes mellitus requiring therapy	2°	2°	
Death from any cause	2°	2°	2°

1° indicates primary outcomes; 2° indicates secondary and composite outcomes; HRT = hormone replacement therapy; DM = dietary modification; CaD = Calcium and Vitamin D supplementation.

Source: Adapted with National Institutes of Health permission from the June 28, 1993 WHI Protocol, p.24.

FIGURE 2-1 Outcomes for the WHI Clinical Trial.

but also quantify the secondary adverse and beneficial outcomes such as cancers of the breast and endometrium, fractures (especially hip fractures), quality of life, and total mortality. It is defensible to test the effect of CaD on risks of hip fracture and colorectal cancer within the context of a study that has been mounted for other purposes; these hypotheses would not stand alone as a rationale for an expensive trial. The DM branch drives the size of the study, the DM-breast cancer hypothesis drives the length of the study, and the DM and HRT branches generate most of the complexity of the study. Each outcome to be measured is hypothesized to be affected by more than one of the CT intervention branches. For example, DM and HRT may affect coronary heart disease; DM and HRT may affect breast cancer; and HRT and CaD may affect fractures.

Integration of the CT with Other Components of the WHI

The goal of the WHI CT is to test whether the interventions being used will reduce the morbidity and mortality associated with breast cancer, cardiovascular disease, and osteoporotic fractures. The WHI Observational Study (OS) is designed to follow women for an average of nine years. The goals of the OS are to: (1) improve risk prediction of coronary heart disease, breast cancer, colorectal cancer, fractures, and total mortality in postmenopausal women; (2) create a resource of data and biologic samples that can be used to identify new risk factors and/or biomarkers for disease; and (3) examine the impact of changes in individual characteristics on disease and total mortality. The OS can provide quantitative assessments of risk factor associations with major chronic diseases in women and it will enable the calculation of improved risk estimates for cardiovascular disease, cancers, bone fracture, and other disease endpoints in older women. Such information is expected to improve the quality of life of postmenopausal women by facilitating the identification and preventive treatment of high-risk women.

Many women must be screened to determine their eligibility for the CT, and this is costly. The marginal cost of following these women in the OS is small relative to the expense of mounting an independent OS. Thus, it is appropriate to conduct the OS in tandem with the CT.

The details of the Community Prevention Study (CPS) are unknown, so the committee cannot judge whether that component of the WHI will draw on the experience or results of the CT or OS. The CPS would fit well into the overall vision of improved women's health if its goals were to develop lifestyle change strategies in diet, exercise, smoking, and early disease detection that are accepted as national goals and for which major gaps in development exist, especially as pertain to women of low socioeconomic status (SES) and minority women. The CPS could also furnish an infrastructure of trained personnel to aid in carrying out interventions and policies that might flow from the CT and OS.

DESIGN AND METHODS

The committee's examination of the CT design concentrated on two fundamental questions:

- **Can the study design—if no operational difficulties occur—answer the questions it addresses?**
- **If the study design is appropriate, what other threats are there to the successful completion of the study?**

The committee focused on twelve issues central to these questions, which are discussed below. Seven of these issues involve conceptual problems that are built into the design of the CT. Even if all study operations were to proceed without incident, these conceptual issues threaten the validity of the findings:

- factorial design
- sample characteristics
- proposed analytic techniques
- ethics: consent and stopping rules
- minority analysis plan
- specificity of intervention and effect
- outcome definition and measurement

In addition to these conceptual problems, any study—no matter how well designed—is subject to setbacks by operational problems. The CT is particularly vulnerable to such problems because of its size, complexity, and duration. The committee has identified five operational issues that could jeopardize the study's success:

- recruitment and retention
- adherence
- secular trends
- provision of health care services to participants
- study management

In the ensuing discussion of these twelve issues, certain specific suggestions are made. More global recommendations will be discussed at the end of this chapter.

Factorial Design

NIH argued that conducting a partial factorial design would reduce the required number of women and attendant costs and allow assessment of interactions among intervention branches. The partial factorial design is presented in Figure 2-2, which has been reprinted with NIH permission from the June 28, 1993 WHI Protocol, page 18. The committee feels that the factorial design has serious weaknesses. The factorial design is criticized because the difficulty of maintaining adherence to one intervention, such as DM, is magnified greatly in a design that requires adherence to two interventions, DM and HRT. The 15.9 percent overlap between the DM and HRT interventions is insufficient to provide adequate statistical power to assess interactions between the interventions. Therefore, the complexity of the design is not compensated by an increase in statistical power.

NIH also argued that it will be more economical for the clinical centers to screen simultaneously for the two branches, DM and HRT, rather than to mount each one separately. As now planned, there are effectively two separate studies, HRT and DM, done within the same administrative structure. It is mostly the efficiency of shared administration which make this plan more economical. In essence, the integrated design has become primarily a matter of efficiency; it is not essential to hypothesis testing.

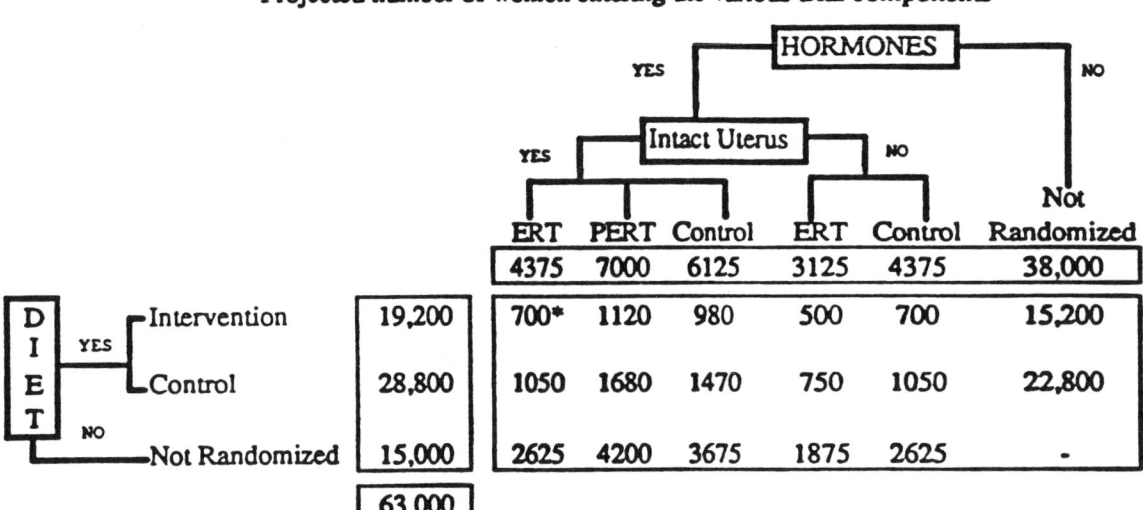

Projected number of women entering the various trial components

*In each cell of this figure appoximately 5 out of 7 women are projected to be willing to be randomized to receive calcium and vitamin supplementation (50%) or placebo (50%), while the remainder will not enter the calcium/vitamin D trial component.

Source: Used with the permission of the National Institutes of Health from the June 28, 1993 WHI Protocol, p.18.

FIGURE 2-2 Women's Health Initiative Clinical Trial partial factorial design.

Sample Characteristics

Size

The CT is one of NIH's largest clinical trials: 63,000 women are expected to enroll. The large sample size is one of the primary reasons that the CT is expensive: the CT and OS are expected by NIH to cost approximately $586 million.

The sample size is driven by the choice of endpoints. The primary endpoints of the CT are incidence of breast cancer, colorectal cancer, CHD, and hip fractures. Because the incidence rate of each outcome differs, and because the study interventions have different hypothesized effects, setting sample size requirements for the overall CT is a complicated task. The cost of the trial, strongly linked as it is to sample size, would vary based on assumptions made. In reviewing the WHI Protocol, the committee was concerned about a number of the assumptions. For example, a continuing linear decline of CHD mortality is assumed; this should be examined in more detail, especially by age group.

For each of the main hypotheses in the CT, the sample size is also determined by the need to achieve a specified power to test the effect of the intervention at a given significance level. Take, for example, the DM intervention. To test whether the difference in breast cancer event rates in the intervention and control groups is an effect of DM, a significance level $\alpha = 0.025$ and a one-sided test is used in the WHI Protocol. The power to test for effects, and hence the required sample size, depends on assumptions made by NIH about the following factors:

- *Age distribution.* Women aged 50-54, 55-59, 60-69, and 70-79 are to be enrolled in the ratio 2:4:9:5, by design.
- *Loss to follow-up.* For the breast cancer endpoint, loss to follow-up is assumed to be 3.0 percent per year due to deaths from other causes or disappearance.
- *Adherence.* Based on the Women's Health Trial Vanguard Study (Henderson et al., 1990), it is assumed that the average percentage of calories from fat will drop from 39 percent at baseline to 20.9 percent at six months, will increase to 21.6 percent at one year, and to 22.6 percent at two years. It is then assumed to increase linearly to 26 percent at 10 years (June 28, 1993 WHI Protocol). For the control group, average percent calories from fat is assumed to decrease linearly from 38 percent at baseline to 34 percent at 10 years.
- *Magnitude and Lag of Dietary Effects.* Based on international correlations between dietary fat disappearance data (rate of use or wastage in the population) and breast cancer incidence rates (Prentice et al., 1988), the WHI Protocol assumes that the risk ratio decreases linearly from RR = 1.0 at baseline to RR = 0.5 at 10 years for fully adherent women. When this effect is averaged over nine years and nonadherence is taken into account, it is projected that the DM effect is a 14 percent reduction in breast cancer incidence.
- *Incidence Rates.* The protocol uses published age-specific incidence data from the SEER program for the years 1985-1989. The resulting percentage of cases, assuming 14 percent DM effect, are 2.92 percent and 2.52 percent for the control and intervention groups, respectively, after nine years.

With the above assumptions, the WHI Protocol states that the power of the test is 86 percent based on a sample of 48,000 women.* It should be noted that the power of the test, and hence the required sample size, can vary drastically depending on changes in the above assumptions. For example, if the intervention effect is only 11 or 12 percent, rather than the expected 14 percent, then the power of the test would drop to 63 or 75 percent for a sample of 48,000 women. In fact, the protocol shows that reasonable changes in just three of the underlying assumptions—follow-up, effect size, and number of enrollees—produce enormous variation in the power, which could be as low as 25 percent (six years follow-up, 11 percent intervention effect, and 42,000 participants) or as high as 89 percent (nine years follow-up, 14 percent intervention effect, and 54,000 participants). All are within reasonable ranges of assumptions.

To illustrate the effect of additional assumptions on sample size, the committee considered an example given by Lakatos (1988). In this example, when the lag time (the interval needed to achieve full intervention effect) increases from instantaneous (zero years) to one full year, the sample size needed to achieve 90 percent power at $\alpha = 0.05$ (two-sided) can increase more than fourfold. Thus, the necessary sample size is very sensitive to the assumed timing of effect on the relative risk.

The proposed protocol assumes a linear halving of the risk over five years. The existing data neither support nor contradict this claim, but the biology of breast cancer would seem to make this an optimistic projection. If diet does have an effect on breast cancer, but the lag time for halving the risk is, for example, 20 years, then the currently proposed project has very little chance to detect an effect. The uncertainty of the lag effect is crucial to the reliability of the sample size estimates. Short lag times would enable results to be acquired more quickly and longer lag times would likely preclude a result in the trial as planned. Information gained in the first five years of the WHI may be critical in setting bounds on these estimates.

Recruitment

Because the sample size determines what recruitment efforts are required, it is necessary to assess recruitment assumptions. The June 28, 1993 WHI Protocol estimates that 33 percent of the 189,000 women who are expected to attend the first screening visit are expected to enter the CT. The CT will randomize 25,000 women to the HRT component (40 percent of whom are expected to agree to be in the DM component as well); 48,000 women to the DM component (21 percent of whom are expected to agree to be in the HRT component as well); and 45,000 women to the CaD component (71 percent of the total), all of whom will be participating in at least one of the other components.

---

* This is based on a modified version of a program designed by Lakatos (1988).

Each Vanguard Clinical Center expects to enroll 336 women in the HRT arm; 846 in the DM arm; 224 in both the HRT and DM arms; and 2,220 women in the OS. As currently planned, each Clinical Center is expected to enroll 39 women per month. Therefore, for each month ahead of schedule a clinic becomes, there is a gain in power from the increase of three person-years (39 person-months) of follow-up. Similarly, for each month a clinic falls behind in recruitment, three person-years of follow-up are lost. Because of the recent delay in bringing on the 29 additional clinics, several months of follow-up are already lost to the study. This delay threatens the power and sample size computations, adding to the level of uncertainty.

Participant Characteristics

Postmenopausal women between the ages of 50 and 79 will be invited to join the CT. It is the goal of the WHI to have the study sample represent initial age categories in the following allocations:

- 50-54 years old—10 percent
- 55-59 years old—20 percent
- 60-69 years old—45 percent
- 70-79 years old—25 percent

The WHI is also striving for, but not requiring, a "representative" accrual of participants with regard to race/ethnicity and SES. This will further complicate recruitment, although it will strengthen the generalizability of the results. It is not clear to the committee how this goal would be enforced.

General inclusion criteria for the CT, according to the June 28, 1993 WHI Protocol, are postmenopausal status, with or without a uterus or ovaries; 50-79 years of age, inclusive, at first screening contact; likely to be residing in the study area for at least three years after randomization; and providing written informed consent.

Exclusion criteria include competing risks such as a medical condition associated with a survival rate of less than five years, invasive cancer of any type in the past ten years, or breast cancer (in situ or invasive) at any time; characteristics that could affect adherence or retention, such as alcohol or drug dependency, mental illness, dementia, or current active participation in another intervention trial; and unwillingness to give up current HRT or calcium supplementation. See Appendix A for more a detailed description of exclusion criteria.

Participants will not be categorized by risk for breast cancer, colorectal cancer, or coronary heart disease. This allows a more generalizable study, but the lack of risk restrictions requires a much larger sample size. The factorial design does not allow specific branches to focus on the most efficient samples, such as women at high risk of CHD for an HRT trial or women at high risk of breast cancer for a DM trial.

Proposed Analytic Techniques

NIH has proposed carefully designed and deliberated analytic techniques. A weighted logrank test will be used to test for the hypothesized effects in the CT (Lakatos, 1988). The logrank test is based on the time it takes until the event occurs. If the event does not occur within the observation period, the case is considered a censored observation. The null hypothesis (i.e., that the intervention made no difference) of the logrank test is that the distribution of time-to-events is the same in the intervention and the control groups.

Although a one-sided test with $\alpha = 0.025$ is mathematically equivalent to a two-sided test at $\alpha = 0.05$ (yielding equivalent sample size estimates), the difference has implications for conceptualizing and monitoring the results. The committee, as well as a number of the investigators, feels that a two-sided test should be used.

Statistical adjustments using relative risk regression methods will be used to consider the effects of including other covariables, the ability of intermediate variables to explain an intervention effect, the estimation of full adherence relative risk as a function of time since randomization, and a reliability substudy.

No multiple comparison adjustments are planned for primary endpoint analysis. Subsidiary outcome analyses will rely on multivariate response analyses when appropriate. While it is legitimate to forego formal multiple comparison adjustment, as long as that is clearly stated in the protocol, the practice stands in stark contrast to the proposed use of the Bonferroni adjustment, one of the most conservative adjustments, in the analyses to be presented to the Data and Safety Monitoring Board (DSMB). The Bonferroni adjustment to the significance level consists of dividing the alpha by the number of tests simultaneously performed and using the result as the level of significance for the test. It seems likely, and preferable, for the DSMB to receive uncorrected data.

Data Safety and Monitoring Board

As in many blinded NIH studies involving human participants, there will be a Data and Safety Monitoring Board (DSMB) with oversight responsibilities. To address the tasks of the DSMB, plans for interim analysis have been drafted. The committee was told that the Clinical Coordinating Center will present data on primary, subsidiary, and intermediate outcomes to the DSMB after Bonferroni adjustments for multiple comparisons are made. Each CT branch will be monitored for early stoppage based on summary measures of benefits and risks. Since the DSMB will have the responsibility of stopping a CT branch if adverse effects produce a risk to participants, these interim plans are not well enough formulated to be adequate. These plans are extremely complicated and are slated to be addressed by the DSMB. This onerous task has major implications. If certain monitoring plans are adopted, it might be decided to provide the participants with some study results. Alternatively, using the severe corrections for all the multiple comparisons, key results may be obscured, delaying the release of important public health results. The DSMB will no doubt address these issues, but the lack of information on how these decisions will be made over the duration of the trial increases the uncertainty about the ability of the CT to achieve specific goals.

The committee suggests that the DSMB prespecify a number of outcomes and situations to monitor concerning stopping the trial.

Ethics: Consent and Stopping Rules

Any clinical trial must incorporate adequate protection for the well-being and self-determination of human participants. This study has such a broad population base and such high visibility that its procedures in this regard are likely to come under special scrutiny. A randomized study is ethically justifiable only when competent professionals cannot discern a reason why one arm of the study is clearly better or worse than others for the potential participants. Allowing a participant to join a randomized trial is ethically defensible only when the participant has enough information to evaluate whether all arms are reasonably equal in her own view or, alternatively, that the differences between arms are of a magnitude and seriousness that she is willing to accept in order to contribute to the common good. After much discussion, the committee decided that it is currently defensible to offer the randomizations to each of the CT branches.

Ensuring that each participant can knowingly accept randomization requires that she know the key information about the risks, benefits, and uncertainties involved, as individualized to her situation. Conventionally, this means that a certain minimum of information is given to the potential participant, who is then encouraged to ask any additional questions that may be of special relevance or interest. Obviously, the respondent to these inquiries must be knowledgeable in the subject area. This information and consent requirement can pose challenges to the achievement of a study's implementation goals.

If the WHI CT proceeds as currently designed, it will require substantial resources to meet the obligation to inform actual and potential participants adequately. This obligation will require much more information about the interventions at the outset, as discussed below, as well as a commitment to provide evolving scientific information over the course of the project.

Informed Consent

The committee found the proposed informed consent measures to be inadequate. The committee was provided with Appendix IV "Informed Consent Guidelines" in the WHI Protocol, approved by the DSMB on June 16, 1993, and feels that the consent forms give no understanding of the likelihood or magnitude of major risks and benefits. Certain women at substantial risk of particular problems would not necessarily learn of the currently known effects of their choice. For example, women at high risk of osteoporosis and/or CHD would not learn from existing materials that HRT has been shown to slow or prevent the acceleration of bone loss (as opposed to fractures), and to reduce the risk of clinical CHD in high risk patients. Women at high risk of breast cancer would not learn that they might increase that risk by using HRT.

The committee's concerns about informed consent were raised with representatives from the Clinical Coordinating Center (CCC) and Vanguard Clinical Centers at its meeting in July 1993. These concerns, when presented to the investigators, were met with three types of responses: that the institutional requirements are higher, that the videotapes will provide the appropriate information, and that the counseling sessions will also provide that information.

Most of the Vanguard Clinical Centers reported that the NIH forms passed their Institutional Review Board without substantial modification. Thus, their institutions are not serving as gatekeepers to rectify the problems observed by the committee.

WHI investigators told the committee that the videotapes being prepared for use at all centers would obviate the concerns expressed. The committee subsequently received the scripts (dated July 12, 1993) for these videotapes. After reviewing the scripts, the committee determined these studywide materials to be unbalanced and inadequate to inform women about their choices. The deficiencies apply to literate and economically advantaged women and even more so to disadvantaged women. The videotape scripts simply do not address risks; on the contrary, their tone and presentation are entirely aimed at reassurance and inspiration, and they do not make clear that support would be available for women seeking more information or declining to be randomized. Thus, adequate informed consent would actually be dependent on individual counseling sessions.

Individual counseling, together with the recruitment material, could be a strong and flexible way to ensure truly informed consent. However, ensuring adequate consent for 63,000 women at 45 centers with tight budgets would require focused attention. The counselors would have to be knowledgeable individuals on the "front line," armed with algorithms and guidelines, and, probably, printed and graphic material about known risks and benefits. These persons would need supervision, training, and monitoring. It is not clear that any of the above is included in the CCC plans or in the site budgets.

The investigators must set higher standards than currently exist in the all-study material, including introductory brochures, consent forms, and videotape information. These materials must provide sufficient information about potential benefits and risks to enable most women to make reasonable choices about whether to be randomized. This material should be available in Spanish and perhaps, also, in more conversational English. In addition, case-specific counseling about consent to randomization must be ensured, must be of high quality, and must be monitored. Interactive video programs might be an appealing and effective way to tailor education and decision-making assistance for prospective patients.

The committee strongly recommends that the consent process be outlined more carefully, be implemented well and monitored across all centers, and be evaluated and updated as needed. This is important for ensuring respect for the self-determination of the participants, ensuring the continuation of participants in the study, and maintaining a favorable public evaluation of the project.

Stopping Rules

The CT involves interventions with effects that may occur within a few years (e.g., protection of estrogen against CHD), after at least five years (e.g., protection of low fat diet against breast cancer) or perhaps many years later (e.g., increased risk of breast cancer in women who use estrogen). The inclusion of several interventions with several endpoints in a single trial makes the stopping rules difficult to formulate. Stopping rules are very important because, otherwise, randomized participants may not be informed of changed understanding of risks or benefits in a timely manner.

The very issues that are worthy of studying in a randomized fashion are those for which other kinds of information are likely to become available during the course of a randomized trial, particularly a prolonged trial. As substantial new information becomes available, the question of whether it remains reasonable to randomize new participants must be addressed, usually by a group of experts assembled for that purpose. Ordinarily, if they decide that the new information makes it unreasonable to randomize new participants, then those currently randomized participants receiving treatment under one branch or the other must also be informed and offered the opportunity to select their treatment. Once this is done, the trial has effectively terminated. This is obviously a serious step, and the evidence for taking it must ordinarily be quite persuasive.

In other cases, new information that is insufficient to change the justification for randomization may nevertheless be sufficient to change the decisions of individual participants as to whether they would accept randomization. There is an ethical obligation to continue to inform participants during a trial, by providing information that might change their personal decisions to continue receiving a blinded treatment. This situation arises less frequently, however, and its effects upon the trial are less certain. If additional information causes cross-over or disenrollment of a small or fairly representative set of participants, the effects may be small. If the information causes these changes in a large or highly biased set of participants, the study might effectively be terminated.

The emergence of new information that may require closing a branch of the CT is not unlikely over the next nine years. One branch is at special risk: the near-term effects of hormones on reducing cardiovascular risk factors and event rates may be confirmed early in this project. Other studies, such as the Postmenopausal Estrogen/Progestin Interventions (PEPI) trial and the Heart Estrogen-Progestin Replacement Study (HERS), might provide additional corroboration, sufficient to make it imperative to tell at least women at moderate-to-high risk that estrogens are somewhat protective against CHD and to be able to give reliable estimates of the size of this effect.

The committee believes that such information must be shared with the participants in order for them to make their own decisions about the possible long-term risks of breast cancer as compared with the opportunities to have reduced risks of cardiovascular disease and possibly reduced risks of fractures. Sharing this information a few years into the project might curtail it prematurely. A reasonable response to this likely threat to the study would be to tell women prior to randomization of the current, still uncertain, estimates of the association between estrogen and CHD, and the long-term health risks. The number of women willing to be randomized might shrink, but the threats to completion of the study would be diminished, once women consenting to be randomized despite these risks were enrolled and randomized.

Data and Safety Monitoring Board

The "stopping rule" in the current protocol appears to be based on "all cause" mortality, supplemented by unspecified intervention-specific outcome rates. The committee is concerned that this complex and interlocking study provides even more than the usual substantial impetus for the DSMB to be reluctant to stop the trial or to provide the participants with additional information. Several suggestions were made by the committee, including the following:

- The DSMB should use preexisting or external information to establish a prior probability that internal data then would have the role of confirming. This might mean accepting an earlier "stop" conclusion than would be justified by data arising solely from the CT.
- The DSMB should perform prespecified subset analyses on participant groups especially likely to evidence harm or benefit.
- The committee was told that the DSMB would only receive data if an intervention group in the study was significantly different statistically from control *after* Bonferroni correction for multiple comparisons. The DSMB should be able to do any analyses it feels are warranted and should examine uncorrected estimates of effect.
- The DSMB should review the monitoring of the consent process, especially to confirm the propriety of proceeding in the face of an expected range of new findings with regard to estrogen and cardiovascular disease.
- The DSMB should evaluate prespecified event rates for morbid and mortal potential outcomes, not only "all cause" mortality.

Minority Analysis Plan

A driving impetus of the WHI is to begin to ameliorate the effects of the historical exclusion of women from clinical trials. A parallel situation exists for minorities, men as well as women.

Public statements regarding the CT describe it as explicitly designed to include minority women. In its granting process, NIH issued distinct Requests for Applications for minority centers. The CT goals include an average 20 percent minority recruitment, with the goal of the minority centers set at 60 percent. To judge whether the recruitment and analysis plans for minority participants in the CT are adequate, one must consider what NIH's intent may be in focusing on minority participation. Motivations for increased minority recruitment in a research study include the following:

- The enduring injustice of restricting participation to any one group whose future members will thereby be primary beneficiaries;
- The unfortunate reality that it is only by research participation that some people have access to promising experimental treatments, and the associated inequity of excluding some groups from that opportunity; and
- The possibility that minorities may have differing risks or likelihood of response to treatment, or a differing disease process (which could affect risks and/or treatment response).

The committee concluded that the CT as now designed would satisfy the first two considerations. The assumptions and implications of the final consideration will now be discussed.

Four of the Vanguard Clinical Centers are designated contractually as Minority Centers, representing African Americans, Native Americans, and Latinas. The data from these groups will not allow definitive conclusions, however, due to the heterogeneity among and within the three populations, and due to the small size of the minority sample. The committee notes that parallel difficulties beset analyzing heterogeneity within the white population as well. The anticipated power of the CT will be insufficient to compare individual minority groups to the majority population. The study will be able to observe trends, if they exist, but will probably not have adequate power for conclusive statistical tests. The committee feels that the inability to analyze subsamples should be made clear to groups that are proponents of the WHI precisely because it might be believed—in error—that the study will provide the opportunity to test such comparisons.

Although the intent of the CT is to generalize the data to the general population, it is not clear that there is a uniform effort to stratify the recruitment efforts by SES for the Minority Centers or at the other Vanguard Clinical Centers or additional centers. It is expected, but not necessarily correct, that many of the minority participants will be at the low end of the socioeconomic spectrum. The committee felt that attempts should be made to include the entire range of SES, both for the majority and minority populations.

The available research instruments may well be systematically biased in assigning SES categories to minority populations. For example, some indices of SES incorporate education, income, and occupation; all ethnic groups are assumed to be equal with regard to these factors. However, a considerable difference in income often exists between ethnic minority and white individuals, even with the same level of education and the same occupation. (Potential distortion by gender is eliminated within the study, since the CT includes only women.) In measuring the SES of minority participants, NIH should consider such recognized difficulties. For example, scales have been adapted for use in minority populations that include only education and occupation, not income. If income is to be a variable included in scales or analyses, geographical differences must also be taken into account.

Specifying the Relationship of Intervention and Effect

While the committee understood the constraints that gave rise to the specific design disadvantages, it pointed out several worthy of note so that expectations do not exceed the capabilities of the study design. If an association were to be demonstrated between the DM and decreased risks of CHD or breast cancer, the scientific and lay audience would want to know whether it was the low fat component or other changes in the diet that decreased risk. The CT is not designed to acquire data from which to respond to such inquiries. Any estimates calculated by CT investigators using regression techniques would not be as useful as a straightforward test set up in a randomized design.

If the women randomized to CaD do indeed experience fewer osteoporotic fractures, CT investigators will not have definitive data with which to separate the effects of the two elements. Also, investigators hypothesize potential effects on breast cancer risk in different directions for the DM and HRT. Despite the partial factorial design of the CT, the amount of controlled overlap of intervention subgroups will not be adequate to test interactions with sufficient power. Finally, given sample size constraints, there is insufficient power to test the merits of ERT in comparison with PERT on primary and secondary endpoints. This last comparison is one with substantial clinical impact.

Outcome Definition and Measurement

NIH and Clinical Coordinating Center documents discuss in detail the clinical definitions of CT endpoints. The committee noted two additional endpoint detection problems. The first lies in the uncertain meaning of tiny malignancies detected by mammograms. If, as it seems to be the case, large numbers of these cases are nests of cells that appear to be malignant at pathology but which do not behave as malignant during the woman's lifespan, then it would be important to be able to distinguish who would have experienced invasive cancer. However, based on current knowledge, there is no way to do this prospectively (or even retrospectively). There is no reason to think that the effect of the proposed diet is similar in tumors of both sorts: clinically malignant, or clinically benign but pathologically malignant. If the population of the two types cannot be separated and if the effect of intervention differs substantially, then results may well be misleading.

Second, despite colorectal cancer being of primary interest in the DM branch and of secondary interest in the CaD supplementation branch, there are no plans to detect it systematically. This is especially important with a condition that can progress undetected for a prolonged period. The committee acknowledges that there are no easy solutions, and encourages NIH and the WHI investigators to consider alternate ways for more complete and unbiased detection of colorectal cancer outcomes. Such detection might entail more prolonged follow-up.

In addition, regarding the definition and measurement of endpoints, the committee suggested that additional constructs that will be measured in the course of the CT be examined in connection with intervention-endpoint relationships. Pain, mobility, HRT-associated mood changes, or concern about a possibly unpalatable diet, all influence adherence, disease endpoints, and total morbidity and mortality, both independently and through the same pathways. Furthermore, the quality of life, as measured in part by these variables, may be as important to individual women as years-of-life-gained or lost.

Recruitment and Retention

General Issues

The recruitment plans for the WHI CT reflect the extensive experience of the investigators and their recognition of the challenges of recruiting for such a massive clinical trial. A national media campaign, which would serve as a catalyst for the local recruitment efforts, is planned. Production of a variety of studywide materials is well underway, as are local recruitment activities.

Although the investigators expect the national media campaign to begin later in 1993, it is suggested in the WHI Manual of Operations and Procedures that the campaign may be delayed until all 45 clinical centers are operational. The media campaign includes a variety of elements such as public service announcements, a celebrity spokeswoman, and media appearances by the investigators on national media such as "Good Morning America." The investigators correctly note that the national campaign will spark the local campaigns, where the heart of recruitment activity will take place.

A clinic-specific recruitment plan was prepared by each clinical center; the plans have already commenced. Some Vanguard Clinical Centers have established a community network that includes as many as 60 diverse groups drawn from civic, religious, government, and other nonprofit groups. The investigators clearly recognize that recruitment involves development of working relationships with these community groups and the media community, as well as use of a wide variety of strategies such as direct mail and print/broadcast media.

The investigators have decided to produce a set of studywide support materials for recruitment. These include a study logo, a brochure, and four videos—one for use in community presentation or general orientation to the study, and three for use as adjuncts to the on-site recruitment process. In addition, a slide presentation for use with professional groups and a sample press release have also been prepared.

Recruitment activity will be reported by the clinical centers on a monthly basis to the Clinical Coordinating Center, which will monitor and report studywide participant accrual. The investigators have organized a recruitment coordinators' group composed of the recruitment staff from the clinical centers. This group will regularly share information about recruitment experiences by conference call, and will report to the Recruitment and Retention Working Group, which includes representatives from the Clinical Coordinating Center, NIH, and six clinical centers.

Despite these efforts, however, the IOM committee has identified three remaining areas of concern that may have significant impact on the viability of the CT recruitment plan and the realistic costs associated with the successful completion of recruitment:

- The "message" of the study is not adequately developed and may be misleading.

It cannot be assumed that the general importance and scope of the study will be adequate to convey a powerful appeal to the target group. Although some centers have developed an altruistic or family-oriented appeal for their recruitment campaigns, the study overall lacks a clear message and theme. Experience in past clinical trials suggests that a successful recruitment campaign involves presenting the study in a way with instant, easily recognizable appeal to potential participants. For example, the PEPI trial used a "Women Have Hearts, Too!" theme with the queen of hearts logo. Given the size, complexity, and length of the CT, the study's message must be clearly developed in order for recruitment to be successful.

The committee recommends, however, that great care be taken in the articulation of a theme, since media coverage thus far has emphasized only one of the CT hypotheses: low fat dietary pattern-breast cancer. Since this is the weakest hypothesis, it should not be the central theme. An expert public relations/marketing consultant might help the investigators develop an appealing message for the study and spearhead a comprehensive national media campaign. Experience in other clinical trials currently underway with postmenopausal women suggests that this type of strategic planning in the early phase of the study is a wise investment of time and resources. Such an investment produces a message that stimulates national and local attention by increasing the recognizability of the study and its appeal to large numbers of women. It is not clear, however, if the current budget has the flexibility to absorb the costs for such consulting services. One method of saving costs might be to explore collaborative association with other groups in similar efforts. For example, the American Dietetic Association has recently begun a national public relations campaign designed to improve the dietary habits of postmenopausal women.

- The increased percentage of the total population in the over-70 cohort (25 percent of the study sample) will affect effort required.

This recent change in the protocol has implications for recruitment, since specialized approaches may be required to attract women of this age group to the study. The degree of experience with this age group varies considerably among the investigators, and only a few Vanguard Clinical Centers have developed approaches for this older group of women. The clinical centers should be encouraged to develop specific recruitment plans for the oldest cohort of women. This should involve sources of recruitment, transportation to the clinical center, and any other considerations that may be unique to this group. The clinical centers should also provide an estimate of the additional costs associated with this age-specific recruitment effort.

- The recruitment plans do not specify if and how the clinical centers plan to adjust their recruitment plans over the long course of recruitment.

Given the very long recruitment period, a general plan for the entire course of the recruitment phase will not adequately address the well-recognized seasonal variations in the community's and the media's receptivity to recruitment efforts. Specialized recruitment efforts will be needed to maintain interest in the study after the study loses its initial news appeal with the media. Experience in past studies has shown that such efforts often require considerable financial support. Additional funds for the CT mid-course recruitment effort do not appear to be included in the current budget, and delays in recruitment decrease the power of the study.

Minority Recruitment Issues

The HRT branch raises many concerns with regard to the Minority Centers. There are few data available on the use and effects of HRT in the minority populations. For example, the effect size for the minority populations may differ from that of the majority population in the study. In addition, the dropout and adherence rates for the minority groups are established on majority group data. Based on the literature, both participation rates and adherence rates are likely to be lower in the minority population than in the majority population. Therefore the sample size for this sector may not be adequate.

The WHI CT Minority Centers have linked their recruitment efforts to the established networks within the local minority community. Religious and political leaders should be involved in the recruitment effort, as well as local women. In these clinical centers, attention has also been paid to recruiting staff from the target community. There is strong concern that the Minority Centers will probably require considerably more personnel at the community level, which implies that those personnel will not be in-kind contributions from the institution.

The Women's Health Trial Minority Feasibility Study, sponsored by the National Cancer Institute and the National Heart, Lung, and Blood Institute, is currently underway to test the feasibility of the DM component in African American, Latina, and low-income women. This 29-month study, carried out at three clinical centers, is designed to note the effect of a changed diet on blood lipids, lipoproteins, and hormones, and to measure the influence of culture and economic status on the maintenance of a low fat diet. The recruitment goal is 2,250 women between the ages of 50 and 79. Recruitment began in August 1992, and as of June 30, 1993 the study had reached 44 percent enrollment. It is too early in the study to establish whether retention and dietary adherence have either succeeded or failed. Recruitment is approximately on target at one site, lagging at another, and drastically behind at the third due to a natural disaster.

Adherence

The problem of getting participants to adhere to treatment regimes in randomized trials is more or less difficult depending on the nature of the interventions, the size of the study population, and the duration of the trial. The WHI CT is particularly difficult because it involves three intervention branches (two of which involve major lifestyle changes or side effects), a large number of participants, and a very long duration. Elements of the three treatment branches in the CT have been tested separately—the DM in the two-year Women's Health Trial, the HRT in the three-year PEPI trial, and CaD in various smaller randomized trials.

The participants in the Women's Health Trial were primarily well-educated white women who, because of their high risk of breast cancer, were highly motivated to adhere to a low fat diet. This trial demonstrated that such women could reduce the fat in their diet to a level close to the target of 20 percent and remain on that diet with some small amount of recidivism for two years. It is uncertain how successfully low and moderate risk women of a wider range of SES and race/ethnicity, including quite elderly women, would fare on such a diet. The problem of adherence is exacerbated by the fact that changes in diet may affect the entire family, not just the woman herself, and they may involve costs and access issues (to fruits, etc.) that are difficult for poor or elderly women.

HRT has various side effects that can also impede adherence. For example, PERT often results in breast tenderness, breakthrough bleeding and acne. Moreover, long-term adverse effects are serious: the risk of endometrial cancer is increased in women who use ERT, and there is serious concern that HRT increases the risk of breast cancer. Adherence can be seriously affected by news reports of adverse (or beneficial) effects of these drugs. The PEPI trial demonstrated that a population of women who were primarily white and well educated could, with intensive staff effort, adhere to HRT for up to three years.

CaD has few adverse effects and adherence is expected to be adequate. The CT intends to randomize women to at least two and up to three interventions. Maintaining good adherence to any single intervention over a period of a decade is a difficult task. As noted, one intervention—DM—involves lifestyle changes, and a second—HRT—has side effects, some of which are serious. The feasibility of achieving adherence over a period of a decade, among women of varying SES, ethnicity, and age, is of great concern as a threat to the study in terms of cost and study success.

Secular Trends

There has been a trend toward decreasing the fat content of the diet in the United States during the last decade. The figures used for planning the trial express an expectation of a change in dietary fat intake in control subjects participants from 38 to 34 percent of calories from fat over the duration of the trial. The assumptions made by NIH about secular trends in dietary fat may well underestimate the actual decline. If secular trends are greater than expected, the differential between intervention and control participants will decrease, especially if there is appreciable nonadherence in the DM intervention group, unless the intervention participants are similarly affected and decrease fat intake more than expected. If secular trends among the control participants bring less change than estimated, the ability to test the main hypothesis is enhanced.

It is very difficult to estimate these secular trends. The committee noted the considerable diffusion of low fat health messages to the population, due in part to dietary recommendations by the National Cancer Institute; National Heart, Lung and Blood Institute; the American Heart Association; other health organizations; and purveyors of low fat foods. In opposition to these messages are firmly ingrained food habits, advertising, and the availability of high-fat foods to most segments of the population. Therefore, any estimate of secular trends must be considered uncertain.

Secular trends also apply to HRT. For example, if the PEPI trial publishes favorable results, many women may elect to start HRT. This sort of change would seriously impair the ability of the CT to proceed as planned.

Provision of Health Care Services to Participants

Research funding typically does not cover routine medical care. However, the identification in research studies of health problems in participants without adequate health care is a difficult problem, whether or not the study had a role in inducing the problem. The current protocol vaguely refers to a regular source of care.

> If any study test suggests that a health problem needs further study, you will be sent back to your doctors or clinic, who will evaluate the need for further study. ("Consent form for the hormone replacement therapy part of the women's health initiative clinical trial," June 28, 1993 WHI Protocol.)

This is not adequately responsible. At least for potentially serious health conditions, and especially for those conditions that might be linked to the study interventions, reliable referral for effective follow-up is essential. The clinical centers should continue to develop adequate links with reliable community providers and adequate follow-up to ensure that care is available. Once this is investigated, it may become essential for the study to pay for some kinds of follow-up for some poor or uninsured women.

Investigators in ongoing NIH projects involving HRT have indicated to the committee that research staff need to spend "considerable time" discussing side effects, associated apprehensions, and decisions with their participants, both in the clinic and on the telephone. Adequate staff time for these activities may not be included in the WHI contract budget. Participants who do not feel their concerns are being taken seriously may drop out, impairing the chances of the study's success.

Study Management

The management of a project of this size represents an unprecedented challenge. Compared to past clinical trials, the WHI CT involves a large number of centers, participants, and scientific questions. Successful management is essential to ensure that protocols are successfully executed and that the primary hypotheses are tested. This depends in part on rapid and effective communication among clinical centers and between clinical centers and NIH staff.

NIH has developed a detailed subcommittee organization to address the different components of the study, a structure that incorporates many Vanguard Clinical Center investigators and staff (see Appendix G). The committee encourages NIH to enlist staff from additional clinical centers as they are identified. A graphic representation of the study management plan is reprinted with NIH permission, from the June 28, 1993, WHI Protocol, page 55 (Figure 2-3).

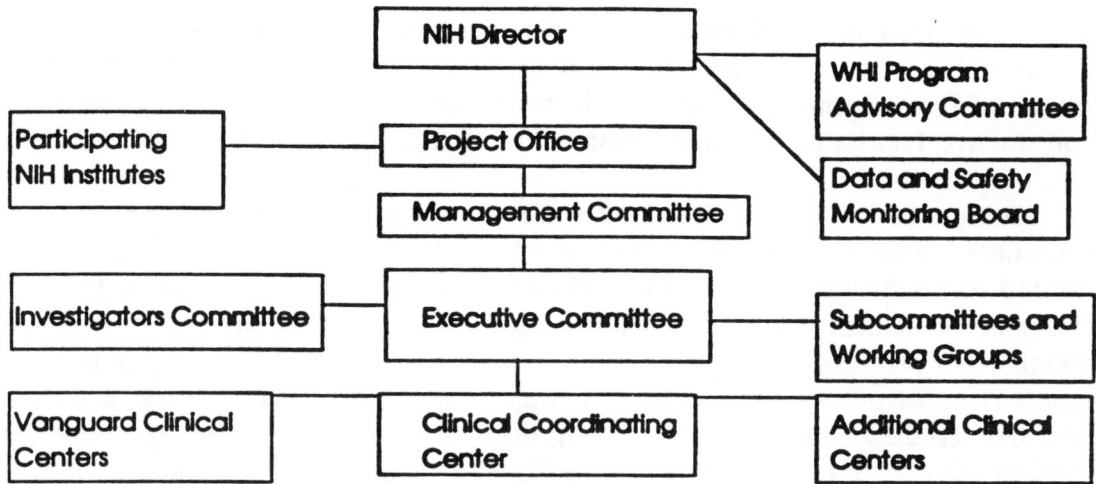

Source: Used with the permission of the National Institutes of Health from the June 28, 1993 WHI Protocol, p.55.

FIGURE 2-3 NIH Organization for the WHI.

DIETARY MODIFICATION BRANCH

Rationale

The DM branch of the WHI CT examines the health effects of reducing total dietary fat to 20 percent of daily calories by reducing saturated fats to less than 7 percent of calories, increasing complex carbohydrate and fiber-containing foods to five or more daily servings of vegetables and fruits, and six or more daily servings of grain products. Each participant will work toward a grams-of-fat-per-day goal based on her weight, height, and activity level. The intervention is considered a "low fat dietary pattern." Endpoints of interest are breast cancer, colorectal cancer, and coronary heart disease (CHD).

Breast Cancer

The low fat dietary pattern-breast cancer hypothesis is based largely on international comparisons: countries with diets of apparently lower fat content have lower rates of breast cancer. Supporting this association are the results of migrant studies in which, for example, U.S. women whose parents emigrated from Japan, a country with low breast cancer incidence, begin to shift toward the higher American rate of breast cancer. However, in the migrant studies it is not clear whether dietary changes, or other changes, were responsible for the increases of breast cancer incidence. In the international comparisons, it cannot be inferred that those who eat the higher fat diets are the ones who develop breast cancer. In fact, many of these studies estimate the fat content of a country's diet by measuring the amount of fat produced and sold; it is not known whether it is eaten by women, eaten by their husbands and sons, used as animal feed, or wasted. Some investigators have shown that much of the international variation in breast cancer can be explained by the variation in reproductive factors across populations. Other factors may also be involved.

In attempts to explain the results of the international and migrant studies, researchers have mounted case-control and cohort studies. Evidence from these types of studies, considered to be stronger in causal elucidations than correlational studies, have shown no associations, or at best weak associations, between diet and breast cancer. Results from prospective cohort studies range from slight protection against breast cancer to slightly increased risks associated with a low fat diet. A recent meta-analysis of data from 12 case-control studies (Howe et al., 1990) demonstrated a statistically significant weak association (RR = 1.4) between estimated fat consumption and postmenopausal breast cancer risk, but three large cohort studies have reported conflicting results. If a low fat diet in adulthood affects breast cancer risk, most epidemiologists agree that its effect is likely to be small. Thus, the low fat dietary pattern-breast cancer hypothesis is considered to be quite weak. In addition, other evidence indicates that nutrients other than fat may be important in the etiology of CHD and certain cancers. The anti-oxidant vitamins (particularly vitamins E, A, and possibly C) are of interest as protective factors against CHD and certain cancers.

There are other concerns with the low fat dietary pattern-breast cancer hypothesis; for example, factors early in life, such as diet during adolescence, may be more relevant to breast cancer risk. Alternatively, the number of years during which the woman ate a high fat diet may be more important in establishing breast cancer risk than intervention on dietary practices later in life.

A strong, consistent association of dietary fat with breast cancer has not been established. To plan the trial, it was necessary to make assumptions based on the strength of this putative association, expected lag between behavior change and change in risk, etc. The committee felt that existing information is not sufficiently certain so as to place the assumptions on firm ground.

Colorectal Cancer

While hypotheses regarding breast cancer risk reduction have focused primarily on dietary fat, hypotheses concerning colorectal cancer include dietary fiber as well. International correlational data between dietary factors and colon cancer are much weaker than the corresponding correlations for diet and breast cancer, although the case-control and limited cohort literature show a stronger strength of association than do comparable epidemiologic studies regarding breast cancer. For example, results from a large follow-up study of nurses indicate a positive association between dietary fat and colon cancer (Willett, 1992). A recent literature review by Potter et al. (1993) notes that a diet high in meat, protein, and fat is consistently associated with a higher risk of colon cancer. There is good evidence that increased consumption of fiber-rich foods reduces the risk of colorectal cancer.

In a meta-analysis of 13 case-control studies, Howe et al. (1992) found similar reductions in risk across gender and age (a marker for menopausal status).

Coronary Heart Disease

There is a strong rationale for a dietary study designed to examine the effects of a lipid lowering diet on various cardiovascular disease endpoints. It is known that a diet low in fat, saturated fat, and cholesterol lowers total cholesterol and low-density lipoprotein cholesterol (LDL-C) levels. It is also known that blood lipid levels are a strong risk factor for CHD outcomes.

While lowering LDL-C reduces the risk of CHD, elevated high-density lipoprotein cholesterol (HDL-C) levels have been shown to be the strongest protective risk factor for CHD. Since a low fat diet, in general, reduces HDL-C, it is important to learn how changes in diet affect HDL-C and cardiovascular outcomes.

In practice, many women, including many elderly women, receive low fat, high fiber diet prescriptions from health care professionals. A study the size and duration of the WHI could add to the understanding of the relationships among diet, its components, physiologic results (such as blood lipid levels), and cardiovascular event endpoints. There have been no major intervention studies conducted in women to address the issue of efficacy of primary prevention efforts.

The weight loss or maintenance of appropriate body weight associated with a change to a low fat dietary pattern could contribute to improved health as well. Decreased rates of obesity could relate to decreased risk of many chronic disorders, including hypertension and hyperlipidemia associated with coronary heart disease. However, significant weight loss in elderly women could possibly have negative effects. Certainly the WHI might provide extensive information about the feasibility of following a low fat dietary pattern and the barriers women encounter in achieving adherence, and the relationship between percent calories from fat and obesity and weight control.

Design and Methods

The research objectives of the DM intervention are to study whether a low fat dietary pattern reduces the incidence of breast cancer, colorectal cancer, and CHD. A total of 63,000 women will enter the CT, of whom 48,000 will be in the DM group and 25,000 will be in the HRT group. About 45,000 of these are expected to subsequently enter the CaD component. The average treatment period is nine years. Post-trial mortality and breast and endometrial cancer incidence surveillance is planned (but not funded) for an additional five years to protect against the possibility of missing any adverse effects that may require a longer period of time to develop.

The DM is well planned and intensive. Women will be assigned to a permanent group of 8 to 15 members led by a nutritionist. They will meet weekly for six weeks, biweekly for six weeks, and monthly for nine months. Individual counseling sessions will be scheduled early in the intervention, and women in the intervention arm will receive nutrition materials as well as self-monitoring tools. While the intervention during the first year is standardized among clinics, there is individual flexibility in actual dietary modification and the rate at which changes will be made. Various other activities are aimed at promoting social support among group members.

The intervention program is founded on theory-based research and past experiences of the investigators. It is expected to lead to the desired outcomes (i.e., the nutritional goals) of the intervention, and the committee was impressed that the investigators will use sophisticated approaches to maximize adherence. However, while the past experiences of the investigators have been successful, there are no data that demonstrate the effectiveness of such a low fat diet over a nine-year period in women of the age-range encompassed in the CT. Furthermore, while many of the investigators have had experience working with postmenopausal women, the literature does not reflect substantial experience with 70- to 79-year-old women following a low fat eating pattern for nine years.

The safety of a low fat eating pattern remains to be established, an issue that is of particular importance in elderly women, for whom many nutritional problems are prevalent. The ability of women with limited financial means to adhere to such a diet is a concern, as well. From discussions with WHI CT investigators, the committee learned that the safety of the diet is an issue of primary importance to the DSMB, and CT nutritionists plan to monitor all intervention women (and pay particular attention to elderly women) for possible adverse effects of a low fat dietary pattern. However, this attentiveness is not apparent in the written WHI Protocol, and the concern is not apparent in the consent process in which participants need to be informed of the need to maintain an adequate caloric intake.

Dietary assessment will be conducted using several different techniques. A four-day baseline food record will be analyzed using the University of Minnesota Nutrition Data System, which has one of the most comprehensive food product and nutrient data bases in the world. It has become the leading U.S. nutrient data base resource for scientific research. A food frequency questionnaire will be collected at selected annual visits on all CT participants. A subsample of these women will be asked to provide a four-day food record. In addition, a subsample will complete a 24-hour dietary recall every 12 months. A semi-quantitative food frequency questionnaire will be administered to women in both the CT and the OS at the first screening visit. The lack of sensitivity of that instrument may seriously underestimate fat intake and thereby hinder recruitment efforts.

Accurate dietary assessment methodologies are essential to the success of the DM. Major sources of error include data-collection methodologies (i.e., the sensitivity and validity of the instruments and methods available); data analysis (i.e., nutrient data base completeness and accuracy); and poor reporting of food intake due to participants' inability to remember total intake, estimate portion sizes accurately, include important descriptors about foods and food preparations techniques, and/or provide truthful information (which is limited for a variety of reasons).

Many potential problems inherent in the collection and analysis of dietary data can be avoided or minimized by having trained nutritionists responsible for data collection and the quality assurance. Moreover, choosing data collection instruments that have been tested widely and using a reputable nutrient data base will also minimize errors and help ensure that the data collected are accurate. The data collected in this trial are likely to be the best possible given the limitations of current, state-of-the-art dietary assessment methodologies.

There is considerable debate in the literature about the validity of these measures. The absence of a clear biological marker for dietary fat makes validity difficult to establish. The trial proposes the use of measures of dietary intake that are state-of-the-art at the present time. It is clear that women in feasibility trials are reporting impressive reductions in dietary fat. What is less clear is the degree to which these reports reflect actual intake. At the present time, there is no viable alternative to self-report techniques.

Weighing Benefits and Uncertainties of the Breast Cancer Arm

Some degree of uncertainty in the hypothesis and feasibility of the methods is inherent in any clinical trial; if one were certain about the outcome, one would not need to do a clinical trial. With uncertainty comes risk and potential benefits. Considerable benefit is gained when assumptions are met, a trial is successful, cause and effect have been addressed, and the public health implications are clear. Uncertainty arises from the possibility that assumptions are faulty and the study hypotheses cannot be tested.

The potential benefits of a study that would demonstrate an effect of diet on breast cancer are enormous. Breast cancer is a particularly frightening disease for women. The existence of a lifestyle change that could reduce risk would be of considerable benefit, both because of the risk reduction itself and the perceived control placed in the hands of potential victims. The primary threat to the DM branch of the CT is that the results will not clearly answer whether diet modification affects incidence of breast cancer. This arm of the study stands in jeopardy if key assumptions are incorrect, and the costs of such an outcome would be enormous:

- A massive expenditure would bring little tangible benefit.
- Funds would have been diverted from other studies that might ultimately have proven more beneficial to women's health.
- Ambiguous results might result in the belief that dietary change is not important to breast cancer, when in fact a link may exist.
- The negative effects of altered diet would be magnified in the absence of clear benefits.

- The failure of this very visible study would erode support for further initiatives in the women's health arena, or in respect to diet effects on health.

Such threats are encountered in any clinical trial and are not unique to the WHI CT. It was the committee's finding, however, that elucidating the breast cancer outcome of the DM contains more than the usual hazard of a clinical trial because of uncertainties of fundamental assumptions. The link between dietary fat and breast cancer is weak and inconsistent. Whether intervention in the specified age group is the most advantageous time for change is in doubt. Whether women will adhere to such a strict diet for so many years is uncertain. Whether secular reductions in dietary fat will be modest is also uncertain.

Because of these uncertainties, there was some disagreement among committee members about whether a trial designed to test the diet and breast cancer hypothesis was justified. The committee agreed, however, that the DM branch of the CT has the potential to test the effect of DM (i.e., decreased fat and increased fruits, vegetables, and grains) on risk of cardiovascular disease and colorectal cancer, and was justifiable on those grounds. Therefore, despite disagreement among committee members over the strength of the scientific evidence supporting the low fat dietary pattern-breast cancer hypothesis, and the feasibility of testing that hypothesis, the committee agreed that the DM branch of the CT could proceed, with the recommendations specified.

The committee also noted that because public expectation is high that this trial will have definitive results regarding the diet and breast cancer hypothesis, NIH should act to limit those expectations.

HORMONE REPLACEMENT THERAPY BRANCH

Rationale

Numerous studies have examined the relationship between exogenous estrogen use and coronary heart disease (CHD), and have generally reported beneficial effects. It is not clear whether the apparent benefits of HRT (from observational data) are due to a process of self-selection by which healthier women are prescribed HRT, or by other selection biases in the inclusion of participants or in the reporting of results. These biases may both exaggerate the apparent benefit of HRT and underestimate the magnitude of adverse effects. This branch of the CT is designed to assess the benefits and risks of HRT on CHD, cancers of the breast and endometrium, fracture rates (especially hip fractures), quality of life, and total mortality. The HRT branch also will provide information on the factors (such as effects on plasma lipids, clotting factors, blood pressure, plasma insulin, and body fat distribution) that may influence the putative protective effect of estrogens on CHD.

Women use estrogens during the menopause primarily to decrease various unpleasant symptoms—such as hot flashes and vaginal dryness—related to estrogen deficit. Other positive and negative effects have been observed, including fewer cardiovascular events and deaths, decreased bone loss, and increased endometrial cancer. Adding a progestin to balance the estrogen restores the endometrial cancer risk to its lower rate. In many women, however, the addition of a progestin causes unpleasant and sometimes serious symptoms.

It is hypothesized that if estrogen decreases bone loss, and bone loss is a risk factor for fractures, then HRT will result in fewer fractures. A critical question is whether HRT increases breast cancer risk. It is unknown whether adding a progestin to HRT increases the risk of breast cancer, attenuates or enhances the estrogen-induced decrease in the rate of bone loss, or attenuates the putative cardiovascular advantage conferred by estrogen.

Small randomized trials have shown that estrogen replacement affects HDL-C and LDL-C levels in directions that would be expected to reduce the risk for coronary heart disease (CHD). The largest proportion of deaths from a single cause in the age group on which the WHI is focused will be from CHD, and therefore the effect of HRT on CHD will greatly influence the effect on mortality from all causes.

HRT with both estrogen and progestin (PERT) has been in common use for a shorter period of time than HRT with estrogen alone (ERT) in the United States, and evidence about the long-term effects of PERT is less certain. Cyclical use of PERT prevents or greatly retards bone loss, although it is uncertain whether the beneficial effect of PERT is greater than that of ERT alone. Any effects of PERT on hip fracture and colorectal cancer risk have not been reported to date. Based on studies of effects of PERT on lipoprotein levels, the beneficial effect of combined therapy may be less than that of ERT alone, although that would be dependent to some extent on the particular progestin used. Whether to use ERT or PERT is an important question among many postmenopausal women and the clinicians who advise them. However, the CT is not designed to test ERT versus PERT.

The effects of initiating HRT at various ages after the menopause have not been well studied. The proposed trial would offer the opportunity to study risks and benefits associated with initiating HRT at older ages.

Design and Methods

In the HRT branch of the trial, 25,000 women will be stratified on the basis of the presence or absence of a uterus. Women with a uterus will be randomized to one of three arms: (1) conjugated equine estrogen (0.625 mg per day); (2) conjugated equine estrogen (0.625 mg per day) plus medroxyprogesterone (2.5 mg per day continuously); and (3) placebo. They will be randomized to the three groups in the ratio of 7:5:8. Women without a uterus will be randomized to one of two arms: (1) conjugated equine estrogen (0.625 mg per day); and (2) placebo. They will be randomized to the two groups in the ratio of 7:5. The percentage of women with a hysterectomy at baseline will be restricted to 30 percent. Power to compare the effects of HRT versus placebo on CHD incidence will be adequate, while the power to detect differences in effects of women in one hormonal group compared to the other will be limited. A variety of exclusion criteria will be applied (see Appendix A).

The committee identified the following unresolved issues with regard to this design:

- The study is likely to terminate early because of evidence demonstrating protection against CHD, thereby precluding the identification of later occurring outcomes.
- Limiting study enrollment to moderate and high-risk women for CHD might maximize the likelihood of early detection of a possible protective effect. A disadvantage would be that the trial likely would need to be stopped even earlier (before the breast cancer association could be learned) because of the greater difference of protective effect on CHD between the treated and control groups.
- The trial would be more informative if the effects of ERT could be compared to the effects of PERT. To do so, the study would need to either increase the sample size, use women at higher risk of the primary endpoint, or change the ratio of participants randomized to different regimens to increase the power of comparison.
- Blinding to the study participants will only be partial because of symptoms associated with the various regimens.
- Knowledge of reported symptoms and the relationship between such knowledge and adherence would be a useful result to come from this study.
- Endometrial aspiration will be done annually on all women on ERT, 5 percent of women on PERT, and 5 percent of women on placebo. Endometrial biopsy will be done only at the request of the clinic consulting gynecologist. The committee is concerned that a 5 percent sample of women on PERT may not be adequate. Also, the committee is aware that some women (with estimates ranging to 40 percent) receiving an unopposed dose of 0.625 mg of conjugated equine estrogen will develop endometrial hyperplasia within one year. It has been suggested that a short course of medroxyprogesterone periodically would reduce this incidence.
- Adherence will be measured by the relatively weak method of pill counts. Alternatives might be blood or urine checks at already scheduled six-month visits.
- It may be more difficult than anticipated to enroll women in this branch of the CT, since many women (or their physicians) will already have decided whether they wish to be on one of these regimens, especially among women in their 70s at randomization.
- Hormones may have different effects on risks for colon and rectal cancers.
- Perimenopausal bone loss requires differential informing of these women and probably also subset analyses that focus upon this effect.

Threats to Completion of the HRT Branch

It is generally accepted that ERT increases the risk for endometrial cancer and decreases the risk for low bone mass. The few observational studies with adequate numbers of long-term users of ERT suggest that the risk for breast cancer is increased somewhat (30 to 80 percent) among long-term users. The effect of ERT on risk for colorectal cancer is uncertain.

The increased risk of endometrial and breast cancer among women on ERT is also an ethical concern, especially since women at high risk for these cancers will be randomly assigned to this treatment group. It is reassuring that they will be followed more closely. Nonetheless, it is important for these women to be fully informed of the risks of HRT during the informed consent process.

Since PERT has been in common use for a shorter period of time than ERT, evidence about the long-term effects of this regimen is less certain. In addition, the effects of starting these hormonal regimens at various ages after the menopause have not been well studied. At present women and their doctors are often making HRT decisions with conflicting information. The proposed trial would offer the opportunity to study risks and benefits associated with initiating HRT at different ages. Given the importance of HRT to a large number of women, work in this area should be a high priority.

Successful completion of this branch of the WHI CT will require a great deal of effort to ensure an acceptable level of adherence with the HRT regimen. In addition, it will be important to minimize cross-over between the treatment and control groups during the trial. There is concern about both of these major potential threats to the successful completion of the HRT branch. With respect to adherence, it is unclear whether women will tolerate the side effects of HRT. This is an especially important point for the older cohort, for which there are no adequate data. These women may be more sensitive to the side effects of HRT and less tolerant of them. A high dropout rate would compromise the integrity of this branch of the CT. Another important concern deals with probable "drop-ins" from the control group initiating HRT due to new scientific findings during the scheduled course of the WHI. For example, the results of the highly visible PEPI trial are forthcoming and likely will have a significant impact on medical practice. Depending on what the results of PEPI are, there could be an appreciable control group contamination, which would confound the findings of the CT.

It is also likely that some women in the intervention group will change their hormone replacement formulations, upon the advice of their own physicians, as a result of side effects or new information, and thus will cause a contamination of the intervention group. Should this happen with a sizeable number of women in the intervention group, the results of the HRT branch would be uninterpretable.

While the issues of dropouts and drop-ins are a potential threat to the successful completion of the HRT branch, it is important to appreciate that there are no data to predict the magnitude of this potential problem. The WHI will thus provide important information about adherence with HRT regimens in women aged 50-79. Finally, it is likely that the effect of ERT on CHD will be seen before the scheduled completion of the CT. The participants of the study should be informed of this finding and asked whether they wish to continue their participation. Given this option, there is concern that this branch of the trial will be discontinued and the effects of HRT on cancer risk will be unable to be assessed.

Use of HRT in Elderly Women

The committee does not believe that the WHI Protocol addresses sufficiently the risks versus the benefits of initiation of HRT in the older study cohort (70-79 years). Therefore the committee presents a more extensive literature review in this section than in the other sections. Among the issues of interest with respect to the introduction of estrogens in an elderly population are several that are reasons to include the elderly in the HRT branch. The committee urges NIH to carefully examine those of the following issues that are amenable to analysis in the WHI trial:

- Will estrogens still be of value in patients with a high degree of osteoporosis?
- Will they afford protection against age-associated cardiovascular disease?
- Are ERT and PERT tolerated by the elderly?
- Will ERT and PERT increase the risk of thromboembolism in an age group already vulnerable to thromboembolism?
- Will ERT and PERT increase the risk of breast cancer in this age group?
- Will the benefits outweigh the potential risks?
- What dose(s) of conjugated estrogens should be used in the elderly?

Osteoporosis

The effect of estrogens in the elderly has been studied by a number of investigators. Quigley et al. (1987) found that patients who begin estrogens in the early postmenopausal years or even in the seventh decade of life will continue to receive benefit with continued use. Those who have never used estrogens until the eighth decade may or may not benefit, depending, probably, upon how much estrogen-dependent bone they still have to lose. Overall, the mean percentage decrease in bone density per year was low in women over the age of 70, and the decrease was similar in estrogen users and nonusers. Adverse events were not discussed. The authors recommended that a double-blind placebo-controlled study be performed in women over the age of 70 to answer the question of whether initiation of ERT would be useful in this group.

In a placebo-controlled trial, Christiansen (1991) observed an increase in bone mineral content in women aged 70 and over treated with estradiol plus norethindrone acetate, versus a decrease in bone mineral content in the placebo group. The effect was greater in trabecular than in cortical bone. Adverse events were not discussed.

A dose of 0.625 mg of conjugated estrogens has been found to be effective in postmenopausal women for prevention or treatment of osteoporosis. Some investigators feel that .3 mg together with calcium is sufficient for women over the age of 70, while others feel that as much as 1.25 mg is required. A dose of 1.25 mg in the elderly may not be advisable, however, because of possible adverse effects on clotting factor and symptomatic side effects.

Morbidity, Mortality, and Potential Risks of HRT

There do not appear to be any systematic studies on whether estrogen used *for the first time* after the age of 70 is associated with any change in cardiovascular risk or overall mortality. Data do, however, exist on "current" estrogen users and ever-users. For example, in a report on cognitive function in a cohort of 800 estrogen users and non-users aged 65 to 95 years (mean 77 years), Barrett-Connor and Kritz-Silverstein (1993) mention that women using ERT had an age-adjusted risk of death of 0.75 compared with nonusers. Most studies of postmenopausal estrogen users have found a decrease in cardiovascular events or all-cause mortality as compared with nonusers. These are summarized in review papers by Stampfer and Colditz (1991) and Wren (1992). However, in two studies, examination of cardiovascular events or all-cause mortality in elderly women showed no clear-cut advantage and, perhaps, an increased risk of cardiovascular events. Bush et al. (1983) reported a significant overall advantage in all-cause mortality in white female estrogen users aged 40 to approximately 79. This was also true in the 70-79 year age range (RR = 0.68). However, in the non-hysterectomized, non-oophorectomized subfraction of the 70- to 79-year-olds (which constituted 56 percent of this age range), the relative risk was higher (1.6) in estrogen users than in nonusers. It is possible that hysterectomized and oophorectomized women began estrogens at an earlier age than non-hysterectomized women, and perhaps the beneficial cardiovascular effects in the oophorectomized women outweighed any potential risks from the estrogen effects on blood clotting factors.

In an analysis of women 50-83 years of age in the Framingham study, Wilson (1985) reported no beneficial effect on all-cause mortality in estrogen users and an increased risk of cardiovascular events, including stroke and coronary heart disease, in estrogen users of all age groups. The risk was somewhat less in the age range of 70 to 83 but there were few subjects in that subgroup. As noted above, most other studies found reduced risk of CHD in estrogen users. The authors speculated that the difference between their results and those of others may have been due in part to the ascertainment in the Framingham study of unsuspected cases of myocardial infarction. (Thirty-five percent of the myocardial infarction cases were clinically unrecognized but were observed by changes in ECG from previous readings). In addition analysis of "interval use" of estrogens was used as compared with cross-sectional classification.

Women taking oral contraceptives are at increased risk of myocardial infarction, stroke, and venous thromboembolism, due probably in large part to the effect of estrogens on blood clotting factors and, perhaps, also to the decrease in HDL-C from the progestogen component and an increase in blood pressure from the estrogen component. The risk is greatest in those with underlying cardiovascular risk factors, especially smoking, and the risk increases with age.

In postmenopausal women with lower levels of estrogen, HRT should pose a lesser risk than in premenopausal women. There have been a number of papers on clotting factors in postmenopausal women receiving estrogens. Stangel et al. (1977) reported low antithrombin III activity in 57 percent of postmenopausal women receiving estrogen, as compared with 15 percent of those not using estrogen. The dose of estrogen (1.25 mg conjugated estrogens) was, however, high by current standards. In a review paper, Wren (1992) noted that although several groups reported an increase in various clotting factors with 1.25 mg conjugated estrogens, other studies reported no differences in various clotting factors between estrogen users (0.625 mg to 1.25 mg conjugated estrogens) and nonusers. This was postulated to be due to a spontaneous increase in antithrombin III and other anticlotting factors with increasing age, thus negating any possible adverse effect of estrogens. In a case-control study of women between ages 48 and 87 (mean 65) who experienced venous thrombosis, Devor et al. (1992) reported a similar incidence of current estrogen use in cases (5 percent) and in controls (6 percent). The study had the power to detect only a twofold or greater risk.

Some women appear to be very sensitive to the clotting effects of estrogen. In addition, some older women appear to have a surprisingly ample degree of estrogenic activity. It is possible that, in these women—particularly if they are obese, smokers, sedentary, diabetic, hypertensive, or hyperlipidemic—administration of estrogens may sufficiently increase the risk of thrombotic events to counteract the salubrious effect of estrogens on HDL- and LDL-cholesterol and vascular endothelium. (The same caveat applies to younger postmenopausal women as well; the same dosage is typically dispensed by physicians and will be administered in the WHI regardless of age and body size.)

Finally, elderly women experience a higher incidence of unacceptable breast tenderness and breakthrough bleeding when estrogens are administered than do younger postmenopausal women. These side effects may cause women to drop out of the CT; clinical staff should be aware of these issues and respond to participants' concerns appropriately. It may be that elderly women require lower doses to produce a given estrogenic effect than do younger postmenopausal women.

Summary

Studies conclusively demonstrate that estrogen therapy has a positive effect on bone mineral density in younger postmenopausal women, and that this effect continues with continued use into the elderly age range. Data also strongly suggest a positive effect on cardiovascular disease in younger and older postmenopausal women. Some elderly women may experience a benefit on osteoporosis from introduction of estrogens if they have sufficient estrogen-dependent bone remaining. It is, however, unknown whether introduction of estrogens in the elderly will result in a positive or negative effect on cardiovascular events and mortality. Also, the relative magnitude and timing of these effects remain fairly uncertain. Thus, the CT will serve an especially important role in helping to elucidate the benefits and/or risks of HRT in women over the age of 70.

CALCIUM AND VITAMIN D SUPPLEMENT BRANCH

Rationale

There is some evidence that the use of calcium in the form of supplements reduces the risk of osteoporosis and resulting fractures, which are serious causes of morbidity for older women. Approximately one-third of cortical bone and one-half of trabecular bone is lost through osteoporosis in postmenopausal women. The rates of bone loss may reach three to five percent per year immediately following menopause, and one percent per year in older women. Although fractures are not a major overall cause of mortality, death from complications of hip fractures (such as thromboembolism, fat embolism, pneumonia, and surgical deaths) are high, and fractures account for much morbidity and dysmobility. The annual incidence of fractures is 0.5 percent of women aged 55-64, doubles to 1 percent of women ages 65-74, and more than doubles again to 2.3 percent in women aged 75-84. Hip fractures will be the primary endpoint for the CaD branch of the CT.

Most women do not have an adequate daily intake of calcium. Postmenopausal women require 1,500 mg per day, yet 75 to 80 percent of women have daily intakes below 800 mg per day (1984 NIH Consensus Conference, referenced in the June 28, 1993 WHI Protocol). The intestinal absorption of calcium declines with age, increasing the probability that calcium in the diet is insufficient to prevent bone loss.

Some investigators have found that the addition of vitamin D increases the effect of supplemental calcium on the prevention of bone loss. It is uncertain if this is because the absorption of calcium is enhanced, or if vitamin D exerts an independent effect on bone (Dawson-Hughes et al., 1991, referenced in the June 28, 1993 WHI Protocol). A subsidiary aim of the CaD branch will be to test the effect of supplementation on bone mineral density. Bone mineral density measurements will be made at only three Vanguard Clinical Centers (it is unclear how many of the additional clinical centers will measure bone mineral density). Changes in bone density over the course of the study will be examined in relation to each branch of the CT.

The CaD branch of the CT is not the primary motivator for the WHI, and it could not stand alone as the justification for the trial. However, it can be justified as part of the CT. In addition, it may provide valuable information on the interaction of CaD supplementation and the DM and HRT interventions. For example, estrogen is known to increase intestinal calcium absorption (as well as reduce renal calculi formation). Therefore, it may be possible to test the hypothesis that HRT and calcium together protect women from osteoporosis. In contrast, low fat diets are frequently low in calcium because of the reduction of dairy foods, and although a reduction of calcium has not been seen in the feasibility studies for the WHI, it will be useful to have a subsample of women in the DM who are also taking calcium.

Colorectal cancer may be related to intake of calcium, and will be a secondary endpoint for the CaD branch. The association between calcium, vitamin D, and colon cancer has also been studied in several correlation, case-cohort, and control studies. The evidence is mixed, with some studies suggesting inverse associations between calcium intake and colon cancer, and others showing no association. Fewer studies have focused on the role that vitamin D plays in colorectal cancer risk, but a strong association has not been identified. It is of course not possible to separate the effects of calcium and vitamin D when they are issued together.

Many women of all ages are currently taking calcium supplements. A clinical trial in which definitive results are provided is necessary for women and their physicians to make informed choices, particularly if responsive subgroups can be identified, such as women who are and are not on HRT.

Design and Methods

Women who are already randomized to the HRT and DM branches will be asked at their one-year anniversary if they are interested in joining the CaD supplementation branch. It is anticipated that 45,000 of the 63,000 women in the CT will be randomized in a 1:1 ratio to either (a) calcium carbonate containing 1,000 mg elemental calcium per day plus vitamin D_3 400 International Units per day, with meals (dispensed as two tablets, each with 500 mg elemental calcium plus 200 IU vitamin D_3), or (b) placebo dispensed as two tablets. Participants and clinic staff will not be told who is in which group.

Outcome information on hip fractures will be collected by annual mailed questionnaires and at all follow-up visits, and documented primarily by X-ray report and discharge summary. Outcome information for other fractures will be collected by annual mailed questionnaires and at all follow-up visits with self-report, and documented by a physician's diagnosis or hospital discharge summary. Outcome information on colorectal cancer will be collected by annual mailed questionnaires and at all follow-up visits, and will be documented by medical report.

The committee is concerned about the inability of this branch to separate the effects of calcium and the effects of vitamin D. Several documents sent to the committee by the NIH provide a fragmented picture of the process through which the decision was made to do only a two-way randomization (CaD versus placebo). The minutes of the Concept Review group for the CT/OS Component of the WHI reflect mixed views in the 10-person panel, and recommend that the NIH planning group "reconsider the question of a 3-group versus 2-group design and assess power for combined fractures and hip fractures." At an advisory meeting on August 15, 1991, the participants strongly encouraged a three-way randomization (calcium, calcium and vitamin D, or placebo). This would permit assessment of whether vitamin D made an independent contribution, although the magnitude of the effect of vitamin D given alone would not be known in this trial.

In February 1992, NIH considered the statistical implications of a three-way randomization.* The authors assumed that the fracture rate is reduced by 30 percent when either calcium alone or vitamin D alone is used, and that adding vitamin D to calcium would increase the effect an additional five or ten percent. With the designed sample size there would be insufficient power to test this well. Therefore, the statisticians recommended not using a full factorial design for this component.

While acknowledging that the practical elements of power, sample size, and cost are necessarily limiting issues, the committee is concerned that the decision to forego testing a three-way randomization was based, apparently, on statistical expediency. There is no evidence provided that NIH considered increasing the sample size of this branch, which could be considered relatively inexpensive since there would be many CT participants not already in the CaD test.

Threats to Successful Completion of CaD Branch

As was discussed above with regard to DM endpoints, colorectal cancer will not be detected systematically in the study. Its detection will rely on information from follow-up visits.

Although compliance is expected to be adequate, it is also quite difficult to monitor. Motivation may be more limited. If a substantial number of pills are not actually taken, the opportunity to see an effect will rapidly diminish.

CLINICAL TRIAL COST

In addressing the issue of cost, the IOM committee considered two different cost components. The first deals with basic accounting: Did the applicants correctly estimate, for example, the cost of one full-time equivalent dietitian? Did NIH check that the applicants correctly multiplied that cost by the number of dietitians to be used? The routine contract-processing done by NIH performs this audit-type function, and the committee chose not to pursue this form of additional audit.

The second—and more appropriate to the committee's charge—cost issue involves whether the Center applicants and NIH assessed appropriately the nature and amount of human and material resources (staff level and distribution, equipment, etc.) necessary to perform adequately the tasks required by the contracts. To determine whether the choices of resources seem adequate, the committee engaged in three activities:

---

*L. Freedman and E. Lakatos, National Cancer Institute, February 11, 1992 memorandum.

- Staff and other expenses were compared across the funded Vanguard Clinical Centers, to see if the distribution and/or outliers might provide clues to consistency of funding and whether problems, if any, were localized or studywide;
- Cost information from other NIH-funded clinical trials was compared, to see whether the relationship between estimated WHI CT costs and work scope was similar to that of other trials; and
- Using personal professional experiences with similar interventions, communities, or endpoints, committee members individually judged whether staffing patterns, intervention components, and overall budget seemed sufficient.

Data Available to Committee Deliberations

The fact that this committee was formed after the funding of the Vanguard Clinical Centers should have been helpful to the budget evaluation, since, rather than mere plans for funding, negotiated contracts existed. However, the task of this committee was made difficult by the repeated failure of NIH to provide cost information in a usable format. For example, NIH considered the institution-specific data on indirect costs to be confidential and insisted that release of that information would affect future NIH negotiations with contract applicants. On the other hand, the NIH did provide average budgets from which to judge some of the issues related to long-term cost assessments.* The Clinical Coordinating Center and some of the Vanguard Clinical Centers were forthcoming, providing specific information about the budget issues. Of necessity, however, much of the analysis of budget was, however based on expert judgment, comparison to other historical and similar information, and the contractual liabilities to which NIH and the Vanguard Clinical Center host institutions had agreed.

---

* On July 28, 1993, the NIH Research Contracts Branch, DCG/OA/OD, issued an amendment to its contract solicitation for additional WHI clinical centers (NIH-WH-93-30 E/W dated July 2, 1993, "Clinical Centers for the Clinical Trial and Observational Study of the Women's Health Initiative—East/West"). The amendment included the cost information regarding the WHI that NIH had provided to the National Academy of Sciences (NAS). It also notified potential applicants that other materials that had been made available to NAS would be available in the RFP Reading Room in the Federal Building in Bethesda, Maryland. The NIH project officer assigned to the IOM study noted that this was done so that the IOM committee members who may be affiliated with institutions applying for contracts did not bring information to the contract application that put their institutions at an advantage.

WHI Cost Relative to Other Large NIH Studies

From the time of its initial contract negotiations with NIH, IOM sought data on the scope and cost of other clinical trials, particularly multicenter, long-term trials. On August 3, 1993, the committee received from NIH a packet of extremely useful scope and cost information, from which it built the display in Appendix H.

In order to gain a quantitative comparison of the WHI relative to other similar, albeit smaller, efforts at NIH, the cost per participant per year was computed from the total costs, total duration, and sample size of 55 NIH studies. These studies were conducted from the 1970s to the 1990s. No adjustments or discounts for inflation were applied. Because some studies provided are clinical trials, some observational studies, some large and some small, some multicenter and some single center, the comparison of costs per participant per year for some studies may be problematic for the comparison with WHI CT costs.

The average cost of all studies for which total costs, duration, and sample size were provided was slightly over $2,300 per participant per year. For studies that were initiated in the 1990s, this figure exceeds $3,000. Information on the cost of the CT was estimated by the Clinical Coordinating Center to be $586 million, consisting of approximately $168 million for the Vanguard Clinical Centers, $142 million for the Clinical Coordinating Center, and the remainder for the 29 additional clinical centers about to be selected. Whereas completed NIH studies include all costs (start-up, trial, follow-up, and close-out), the CT calculation can only consist of estimated costs. To arrive at the estimated cost per participant per year the committee used the estimated average follow-up period of nine years (from WHI power computations) to reflect the person years of follow-up. This number was multiplied by the 63,000 participants to yield the total number of person-years of participation. The anticipated NIH contribution of $586 million was then divided by the resulting 567,000 person-years, yielding a cost per participant per year of $1,034. The costs associated with the OS are not excluded, which makes the estimate conservative in that including the OS participants further deflates the cost per participant per year. For example, if the cost of the OS is $15 million, and this is subtracted from the total cost, the cost per participant per year drops to $1,007.

Comparisons of the WHI costs with those of similar trials yield similar disparity. For example, the PEPI trial costs slightly in excess of $2,000 per participant per year, and the Women's Health Trial (WHT) Minority Feasibility pilot studies in excess of $3,000. Despite the size and complexity of the WHI, requiring a great deal of staff emphasis, the WHI funding per person per year is less than half that for other NIH studies of women's health, including specifically those that use similar drug regimens (e.g., PEPI) and approach (e.g., WHT Minority Feasibility Study).

Clinical Center Funding

The average 12-year budget for a Vanguard Clinical Center is approximately $10.5 million. Appendix I presents the budget as provided by NIH. While the additional clinical centers have not been selected or contracts negotiated, NIH officials told the committee that they expect to fund these centers at lower rates, even though they would be expected to cover the increases in sample size that are now required.*

The average indirect cost rate shown on NIH summary documents is lower than on-campus rates of most universities. The acceptance of lower indirect cost rates implies the institutions will be covering the costs for some services that would normally have been paid for by higher indirect cost rates. Some Vanguard Clinical Center representatives suggested that support for WHI activities provided by their institution is through accepting off-campus rates. None of the centers that responded to the committee stated that their institutions were actually providing the direct 0.23 full-time equivalent support shown in the average data from NIH (however, only a few Vanguard Clinical Centers provided information). Taking these factors into account, the cost per new clinical center could be $10 million.

The investigators in the Vanguard Clinical Centers have made numerous adjustments and attempts at efficiencies in the CT—such as proposing the use of trained volunteers and economies of scale in purchasing—in order to arrive at acceptable cost projections. The committee appreciates the enormous efforts that have already gone into the cost cutting and protocol modifications designed to produce cost efficiencies and savings. Nonetheless, the committee felt that the costs budgeted for the Vanguard and additional clinical centers are low for the extensive effort necessary.

NIH negotiated contract funding amounts with each Vanguard Clinical Center based on estimates of future costs, including an official inflation factor. What is unpredictable in the specific but to be expected in general is that, over the course of this 12-year trial, medical technologies, practice patterns, and pharmaceutical agents will continue to evolve. Past experience demonstrates that these advances are often accompanied by increased costs. The Vanguard Clinical Center representatives did not have a shared view of what would be expected of their projects, their institutions, or NIH, should increased costs impinge on the functioning or quality of the trial. This led the committee to explore NIH funding in relationship to the total cost of the WHI.

---

* The June 28, 1993 WHI Protocol notes an increase based on changes in age distribution, overlap of interventions, and other revised assumptions.

Total Cost

Critics say that all three WHI components cannot be done for the announced costs of $625 million or, alternatively, that the announced costs are excessive. To determine whether there are sufficient resources to carry out the CT, OS, and CPS as designed, the committee also looked at non-NIH sources of funding committed to WHI activities.*

Institutional Support

The direct cost contributions of the contracting institutions have not generally been considered in the critics' costing of the study. The cost assessment must therefore address both the funded and hidden costs of the studies. Institutions have agreed to support the CT to varying degrees, and that support represents real costs to be considered in the committee's assessment. This is not unique to the WHI nor does it represent a departure for NIH in its research funding, but there are also tangible and intangible institutional benefits to giving specific contributed support in order to secure a clinical or coordinating center. It is the extent of these hidden costs, and the financial basis upon which they are to be covered, that is an issue.

The committee has two very different concerns about the apparent expectation of and reliance on institutional support. First, it would like to consider the effects such a policy has on which centers receive NIH research funding. If it is essential that an institution make significant extra-contract support available to a project in order to receive research funding, some institutions are necessarily excluded from the application process, possibly creating an unintended effect of skewing contracts away from very capable investigators who are located at less well-endowed, less established, or more financially wary research institutions. Second, but with more direct relevance to the WHI, the committee is concerned that when seeking additional centers, the NIH might not be able to identify 29 institutions with both qualified investigators *and* the ability to provide substantial institutional support. The Vanguard Clinical Centers are very likely to be more sophisticated and experienced centers, which may enable them to be more efficient and have more resources with which to support the efforts of the trial. Will the forty-third, forty-fourth, and forty-fifth centers chosen have the experience to carry out the tasks of high quality research with very limited resources? If not, the overall quality of the WHI is threatened. In that context, this issue falls under this committee's domain.

Changes in Scope of Work

A related issue is the extent to which the investigators understand these institutional commitments. There was a diversity of opinion among the Vanguard Clinical Center

---

* Staff effort at the NIH Office of the Director, NHLBI, NCI, and ORWH has been substantial and is not accounted for in the WHI $625 million budget.

investigators as to what the contract actually requires financially in terms of anticipated or unanticipated changes in the sample size, scope of work, etc. This must be clarified. For example, if several years into this project a PI faces greater expenses than were budgeted, how will this be handled? Will NIH provide additional support, will the institution in which the clinical center is based provide necessary funding—at the expense of the PI's other projects or from general funds? Or will the quality of work on the WHI tasks suffer? Some PIs believe that by signing the contract, the institution agreed to pick up any necessary additional costs. Others see a more standard contract, in which NIH would allocate more money if the scope of work were to change. What if, though, the scope were to remain the same but the costs increase? Still other investigators assume that NIH would not allow its investment to founder and would provide additional funding if necessary.

Ancillary Studies

The committee recognizes that Vanguard Clinical Center investigators and others have plans to request funds—from NIH and other public and private sources—to carry out studies ancillary to the WHI. Although adding in the funding amounts of those studies would increase the total cost associated with the WHI, the committee believes ancillary studies represent anticipated and desired side benefits to such a large trial. NIH has already proposed a mechanism for review of ancillary studies.

Potential Causes of Budget Shortfalls

Despite elegant planning and budgeting, there are predictable threats to maintaining a study of this scope within its budget. These include difficulty in recruiting participants, unanticipated staff turnover, inadequate adherence to the protocol, and larger than estimated cross-overs. As any one of these occurs, the budget will affected; for each additional problem encountered, the budget will be further challenged.

Participant Recruitment

If participant recruitment were to lag, there is no money available for increased—and usually more costly—staff time, clinic hours, or promotional materials.

In response to questions by the committee regarding the ability to recruit minorities and older women and to monitor various demographic characteristics, such as SES and age level, during recruitment and enrollment, NIH pointed out repeatedly that the Vanguard Clinical Center investigators have signed contracts to produce specific recruitment results for the monies allocated. If a clinical center has insufficient funds in reserve to accomplish this, however, it will threaten the validity of the science in a number of ways, but most prominently in diminishing the power of the CT by reducing the person years of follow-up. If NIH plans to drop centers experiencing recruitment delays (the possibility for which has been adequately planned by randomizing within centers), those person-years attributable to a clinical center will be lost, thus weakening the study. These person-years of follow-up can be regained, but only at additional cost by increasing enrollment at other centers and/or extending the study. Thus, if the funding is not adequate to recruit and to implement the interventions with appropriate intensity, the tests of the hypotheses will suffer.

If the informed consent interview (discussed above) were to include, as recommended by the committee, a fuller description of possible risks and benefits, along with estimated probabilities of their occurring for a given participant, fewer women may consent to be randomized. This could slow the recruitment rate or increase the efforts needed to compensate for the higher refusal rate. In either case, increments in costs would ensue.

Staffing

If there is unanticipated staff turnover, the study will incur additional costs. Especially in a 12-year study involving 45 centers, new staff must be recruited and trained, and this will raise related costs. Staff turnover also has the potential to delay recruitment and threaten adherence to the protocols, thus delaying the study with the accompanying financial and validity costs.

Adherence

Similar threats to the budget lie in attempts to achieve adequate adherence to the intervention regimens. If adherence to the DM or the medication schedule is weak, a clinical center could direct increased effort at education and incentives leading to increased adherence. Increased effort would translate into more staff time or more highly skilled staff, both at higher cost. If such additional resources were not available, any potential difference in outcomes between the intervention and control groups would be attenuated because of poor adherence to the intervention regimen and, therefore, the diminished difference in group exposures.

Cross-Over

Investigators anticipate some cross-over of study participants from intervention regimens to control and vice versa. The extent of that cross-over activity is difficult to estimate, especially in a clinical trial involving more than one intervention with potentially problematic side effects. Expected cross-over in the DM branch is exceptionally uncertain, because few studies have attempted dietary change over a 12-year duration. Percentages in excess of the small percentages planned of participants changing their dietary or medication patterns could affect necessary sample size needed to test various hypotheses. To overcome the effect of cross-overs, investigators would need to increase sample size at concomitant expense.

The committee recognizes that NIH has considered many of these threats as well as others. Memoranda from NIH statisticians, for example, note that the occurrence of these difficulties will be monitored and sample size and power calculations would be adjusted as necessary. The committee remains concerned, however, that while such adjustments would be required, the adjustments alone could not ameliorate the effects on the study. Additional source of funding would be needed to maintain sufficient power for meaningful statistical comparisons.

Summary

The committee feels that all three WHI components cannot be done for the announced costs of $625 million. In terms of the total cost of the WHI, with the Clinical Coordinating Center at $142 million, if the Vanguard Clinical Centers are funded at $10.4 million each and if additional centers are funded at $8 to $9 million each, this will account for approximately $570 to 580 million of the $625 million that has been committed before consideration of the funding of the Community Prevention Study. If additional centers are funded at $10 million each, the total committed funding would be, however, $600 million, leaving only $25 million for the CPS.

Are the proposed Vanguard Clinical Center budgets adequate? There is apparently a good deal of variability in Vanguard Clinical Center budgets and in expected institutional commitments. Certainly many of the Vanguard Clinical Center representatives stated comfort with their ability to achieve the requirements of the study for the budget, especially relying on institutional contributions. Some were not as certain. The integrity (and cost estimates) of WHI depend on the collective whole, not just those who are confident.

The committee concluded that the planned expenses are not excessive in relation to the research tasks they are to cover. NIH's publicizing of the WHI as one mega-study may enhance its chances at recruitment and public health promotion publicity. However, this characterization masks the fact that WHI is several studies of lesser cost combined in a single package.

After extensive formal and informal conversations with NIH, PIs, and other Vanguard Clinical Center representatives, the committee gets the picture of a very tightly budgeted trial—if nothing goes wrong. Should things not all go according to plan and estimate, however, there is little room for correction. The committee feels that the majority of the Vanguard Clinical Centers could probably function with the formal and informal arrangements in place but this is probably not true for all of the additional clinical centers. This does not give the committee the confidence to state that the funding of the WHI, as now designed, is adequate.

Because of the many uncertainties, the committee is uneasy regarding whether the budgeted funds will be adequate to carry out the WHI even if nothing unanticipated goes awry. The committee believes that the WHI CT will face enormous difficulties along the lines discussed above. In addition, it is impossible to assess the firmness of the nebulous soft costs that many institutions have committed to over the 14 years, which will probably span different institutional administrations. In sum, the committee believes that the project cannot be fully completed as planned within the current budget.

FINDINGS AND SUGGESTIONS

The committee feels that the Women's Health Initiative (WHI) had inadequate peer review from within NIH or from outside scientists. Although various elements of the WHI were reviewed at one time or another (e.g., the dietary modification trial was reviewed many times in earlier proposals, none of which were allowed to proceed), the committee's impression is that the complicated interlocking combination of the clinical trial and the observational study at the inter-Institute level was not reviewed as rigorously as the usual Institute-initiated project. It seems that this inter-Institute study fell outside the established review process.

- *The committee suggests that NIH reexamine and strengthen the mechanism through which it reviews future inter-Institute proposed projects.*

The committee concentrated on two fundamental questions.

Can the design answer the questions it addresses, if no operational difficulties occur?

If the study design is appropriate, what threats are there to the successful completion of the study?

The committee identified seven issues involving conceptual problems that are built into the design. Even if all study operations were to proceed without incident, these design issues threaten the validity of the findings. Where appropriate, the committee has also suggested strategies to overcome the difficulties.

Factorial Design

NIH argued that conducting a partial factorial design would reduce the required number of women and attendant costs and allow assessment of interactions among intervention branches. The committee feels that the factorial design has major drawbacks. The overlap of 15.9 percent between the DM and HRT interventions is insufficient to provide adequate statistical power to assess interactions, and the difficulties of maintaining adherence to two or three interventions detracts from the attractiveness of a factorial design. In essence, the integrated design has become primarily a matter of economic efficiency; it is not essential to hypothesis testing.

Sample Characteristics

In determining sample size, the study design relies heavily on extremely uncertain assumptions regarding magnitude of effect and lag times. This concern is a factor in the recommendation described below regarding study duration.

Participants will not be categorized by risk for breast cancer, colorectal cancer, or coronary heart disease. This allows a more generalizable study, but the lack of risk restrictions requires a much larger sample size. The factorial design does not allow specific branches to focus on the most efficient samples, such as women at high risk of CHD for an HRT trial or women at high risk of breast cancer for a DM trial, according to NIH assumptions.

Proposed Analytic Techniques

Committee concerns center on choice of endpoints for trial closeout and the planned use of methods to adjust for multiple comparisons when considering interim decisions by the Data and Safety Monitoring Board (DSMB).

- *The committee believes that studywide material must inform potential participants of risks as well as benefits. The committee suggested that unadjusted data be made available to the DSMB. The committee felt that the Bonferroni statistical adjustment, for which current analysis plans call, might be too conservative and therefore might deprive many participants of an appropriately timed conclusion to the study.*
- *The committee also suggested the use of two-sided tests of significance to maintain a scientifically-justified neutral stance regarding whether the interventions might yield beneficial or adverse effects.*

Ethics

The informed consent measures do not provide an adequate understanding of the likelihood or magnitude of major risks and benefits. The obligation to inform potential and current research participants would require much more information at the outset, as well as a commitment to provide evolving information over the course of the project.

- *The committee suggested that the counselors at the clinical centers be knowledgeable and have access to algorithms, guidelines, and printed material about known risks and benefits. These counselors would need supervision, training, and monitoring. In addition, new information from this as well as other pertinent trials (as judged by the WHI coordinators and the DSMB) must be shared with the participants to allow them to make their own decisions about ongoing risks and benefits of the interventions.*

The inclusion of several interventions with several endpoints in a single trial makes the stopping rules difficult to formulate.

- *Therefore, the committee suggested that the DSMB should (a) use preexisting or external information to establish a prior probability that internal data could confirm (this might mean accepting an earlier "stopping" conclusion than would be justified by data arising solely from the CT); (b) perform pre-specified subset analyses on participant groups that are especially likely to evidence harm or benefit; (c) ask to examine uncorrected estimates of effect and do any analyses it feels are warranted; (4) review the monitoring of the consent process; and (5) evaluate pre-specified event rates for potential morbidity and mortality outcomes.*

Minority Analysis Plan

As currently designed, the study will have insufficient power to compare individual minority groups to the majority population. The study will be able to observe differences, if they exist, but will not be able to test them with adequate power.

- *The committee encourages NIH to make these limitations known to those who may be expecting definitive comparative findings among minority and majority groups.*

Specificity of Intervention and Effect

The CT design does not distinguish which element of the low fat dietary pattern may be responsible for any observed outcome. Similarly, the design will not allow analyses to distinguish whether calcium or calcium plus vitamin D is responsible for any observed outcome. Because some endpoints can be affected by more than one of the study interventions, and because the factorial design is modified by participant decisions, the overlap and interactions will be difficult to analyze.

Outcome Definition and Measurement

Threats to accurate and unbiased endpoint detection include the obscure meaning of many mammography-detected tiny malignancies; the unstandardized method of detecting colorectal cancer; and the inadequate development of behavioral, psychological, and quality of life measures for use in the study.

- *The committee encourages NIH to include measures of constructs such as pain, mobility, and psychological status.*

In addition to the conceptual problems described above, any study—no matter how well designed—is subject to setbacks by operational problems. The WHI CT is particularly vulnerable to such problems because of its size, complexity, and duration. The committee has identified five operational issues that could jeopardize the success of the study:

Recruitment, Retention, and Adherence

The message of the study is not adequately developed and may be misleading.

- *The committee suggests that NIH and the clinical centers develop an overall message for the study that pays particular attention to long-term recruitment strategies for older and minority participants, and does not emphasize the WHI as a breast cancer prevention trial. In addition, investigators should set higher standards for studywide materials than currently appears to exist, including introductory brochures, consent forms, and videotape information. This information should be available in conversational language.*

NIH has made overly optimistic assumptions about recruitment, retention, and adherence, especially in subgroups with which researchers have less clinical trial experience, such as older women, minority women, and the spectrum of socioeconomic status (SES) and in recruitment plans that cover many years.

- *Nevertheless, the committee encourages NIH to seek diversity within the sample and suggests that attempts should be made to include the entire SES range in this study.*

The acceptability of the various branches of the CT to women is unclear at this stage, especially since the interventions are difficult and have potential side effects.

- *To maintain adequate statistical power, the CT must have funds available to boost recruitment efforts if, as the committee expects, recruitment rates are lower than anticipated.*

Secular Trends

If secular trends toward a decreasing fat content in the U.S. diet continue, and if there is appreciable nonadherence in the DM treatment group, the difference between the treatment and control diets is likely to be too small to show a treatment effect.

Provision of Health Care Services to Participants

The current protocol includes a referral to a regular source of care. This is not adequately responsible.

- *The committee suggests that the clinical centers must continue to develop adequate links with reliable community providers to ensure that adequate follow-up care is available. It may become essential for the project to pay for some kinds of follow-up for some poor or uninsured women.*

Research staff need to spend considerable time discussing side effects with participants, and dealing with associated apprehension, both in the clinic and on the telephone. To fail to do so is to risk unethical behavior and increased study dropout. The current budget may not include adequate staff time for these activities.

Cost

The committee believes that the total costs of the CT will be greater than the $625 million provided by NIH. NIH and Vanguard Center representatives have indicated that the additional funds necessary for successful completion of the trial will be covered by the institutions at which the Vanguard Centers are based. This reliance on institutional support may be reasonable in the case of the Vanguard Centers, but the committee felt it is unlikely that an additional 29 institutions can be identified that have both the experience to carry out the tasks of high quality research and the ability to provide additional resources.

Potential sources of budget shortfall include lagging participant recruitment, which could require increased staff resources; staff turnover, which could require training and travel resources and might delay recruitment, threaten adherence, and, therefore, affect study validity; and cross-over of participants between study intervention regimens and control status.

The CT funding per person per year is less than half that for other recent NIH studies of women's health, including, specifically, those that use similar drug regimens and approaches.

There does not seem to be a budget adjustment plan for unanticipated changes in either the scope of work or medical technology during the course of the trial.

- *In addition to its concerns about initial funding levels, the committee was concerned about long-term funding and suggested that NIH clarify what the contract requires financially in terms of anticipated or unanticipated changes throughout the duration of the study.*

RECOMMENDATIONS

Finally, the committee was charged to begin with the existing WHI design, consider threats to its successful completion—whether design, financial, or ethical—and to consider whether it would yield reliable results.

- **The committee recommends that the dietary modification-breast cancer hypothesis be considered a subsidiary rather than a primary hypothesis, shifting the emphasis to the effect of dietary modification on coronary heart disease outcomes, making those the primary hypotheses.**

- **The committee recommends that the consent process be outlined more carefully, be conscientiously implemented and monitored across all centers, and be evaluated and updated as needed.**

- **The committee recommends that the CT be scheduled to end in mid-2002, rather than close out the interventions by April 2005, and that the findings of an Objective Prescheduled Reassessment (OPR) be available by April 2002 (see Figure 2-4).**

The OPR, managed through an internal or external review board, would consider whether continuation or modification of the CT could be justified. Recruitment for the CT began in September 1993, so the project would run unimpeded for more than eight years (unless the Data Safety and Monitoring Board moves to stop the trial sooner based on external or interim data). Data analysis would begin in October 2001 and conclude with a recommendation by April 2002. Between October 2001 and the decision to extend, modify, or terminate, the CT would continue in its active mode. Sufficient time would be provided for closeout or redesign and data analyses.

This recommendation addresses the primary concerns of the committee in the following ways:

- Data from nearly six years mean follow-up time would be available for the OPR. According to NIH power calculations (see Appendix J), this timeframe would allow hypotheses regarding stronger, expected associations (HRT and coronary heart disease; and HRT and combined fractures) to be tested and findings disseminated in a timely manner. If the intervention effect is strong, this timeframe also allows the hypotheses regarding the weaker, expected associations (DM and CHD; CaD and hip fractures; and HRT and hip fractures) to be tested. This timeframe does *not* allow for adequate follow-up for the DM and breast cancer hypothesis, the DM and colorectal cancer hypothesis, or the HRT and breast cancer hypothesis. However, the committee feels that, as currently designed, the CT does not have a high probability of yielding statistically significant results for the DM and breast cancer hypothesis or the HRT and breast cancer hypothesis, even after more prolonged follow-up. The committee would therefore prefer to see the other hypotheses analyzed in an appropriate timeframe. While the DM and colorectal cancer hypothesis is reasonable, it alone does not justify continuing the CT.

- This recommendation allows an assessment that would be informed by recruitment, retention, adherence, and incidence experience; if any of these estimates have not been or are not being met, the problem can be addressed. For example, if HRT is demonstrated to be favorable compared with control, the CT could reassign the control participants (with their permission) to ERT or PERT, thus increasing statistical power for that direct comparison, which as designed is not currently adequate. If there is evidence that the DM-breast cancer investigation should continue, justifications for that should be offered at the same time. If recruitment or adherence experience is so poor that an adequate test of a hypothesis would not be possible in any reasonable time frame, the CT or a branch of it could terminate. If, on the other hand, recruitment or adherence problems are discretely identifiable, the study could be redesigned for the remaining duration to compensate for these problems.

- Any clinically beneficial findings of the CT can be made available to participants. Clinical knowledge resulting from other studies can also be applied to participants in both intervention and control arms of the CT. Therefore, WHI investigators would not be pressured to deny benefits to women in the CT to keep intact its overlapping studies.

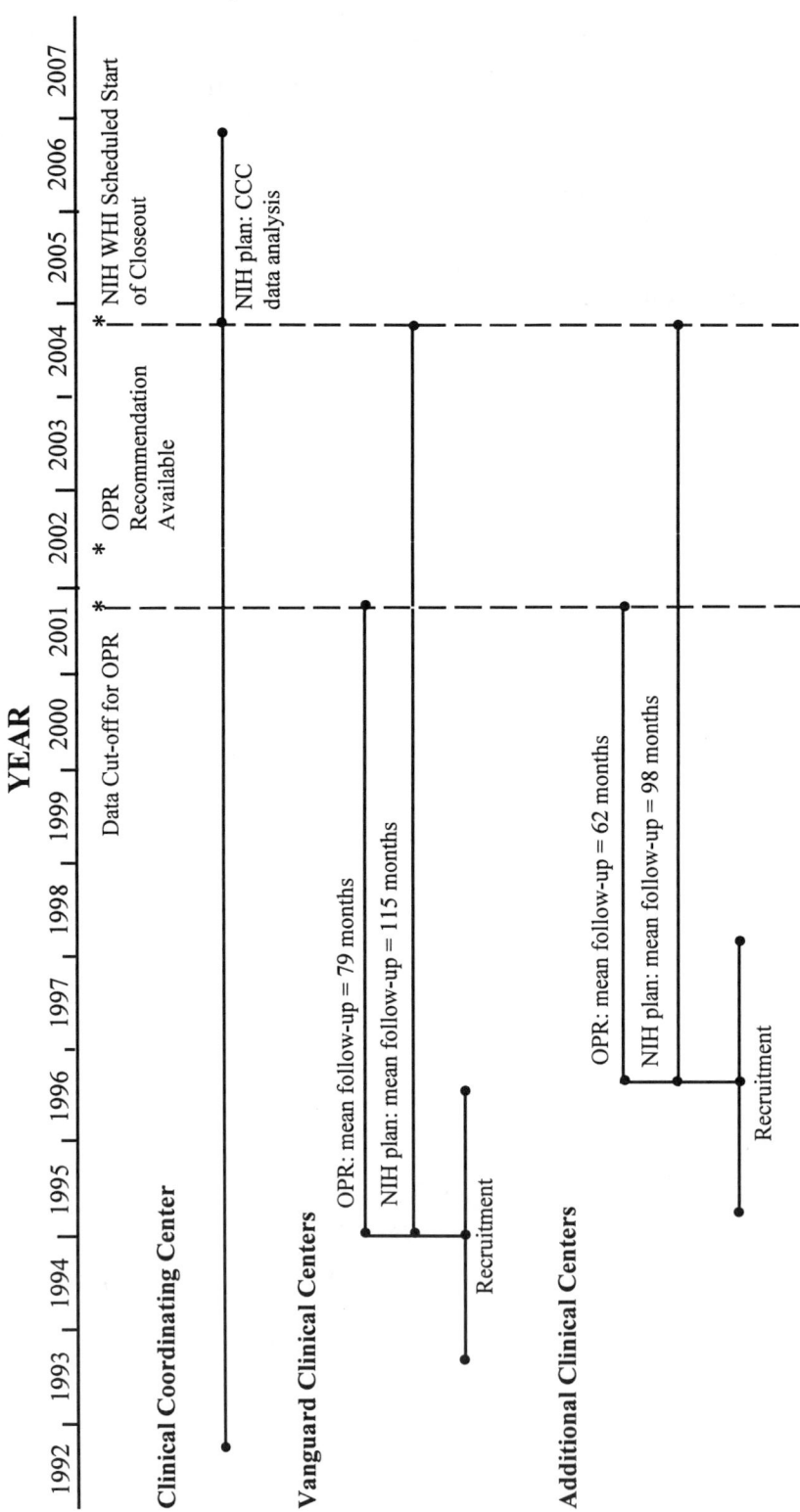

FIGURE 2-4 Objective Prescheduled Reassessment Timeline.

3

Observational Study

RATIONALE

NIH considers the Observational Study (OS) an important component of the Women's Health Initiative (WHI), but it has not given it nearly the amount of attention given the Clinical Trial (CT). The OS will draw from women who have participated in at least one CT screening visit but who are either not eligible or not willing to participate in the CT, and who agree to participate in the OS. It is anticipated that 45 clinical centers will enroll approximately 100,000 women in the OS, following them for an average of nine years. Data collected at baseline are to be related to subsequent clinical events in order to examine the associations of both putative risk factors and protective factors with subsequent disease occurrence. An observational study of this scope would require a very large investment if it were initiated independently. Designed as a WHI component, however, it can take advantage of the baseline information that will have been collected in the course of the screening to form the CT cohort. The marginal cost of the OS—that amount that would be required in addition to what is already required by CT protocol—is therefore relatively reasonable for the information to be acquired.

The OS thus has the potential to complement the CT by providing another (larger) cohort, although one in which hypothesized preventive measures are not assigned at random. Not only could investigators use this cohort to pursue hypotheses related to those of the CT, they would have the opportunity to describe myriad relationships among putative risk factors, participant characteristics, physiologic changes, and morbidity and mortality. Diseases such as Alzheimer's disease, osteoarthritis, and stroke are common, yet much remains to be learned about risk factors. The sequence of events, behaviors, and diagnoses is more readily apparent in a prospective cohort study such as the OS than in case-control studies, diminishing at least some of the difficulties in interpreting results. This longitudinal study presents a good opportunity to be able to better differentiate among antecedents, intervening variables, and effects, thus providing information on predictors of these diseases and others of public health importance.

The committee was provided with a proposed list of variables to be measured at baseline and at the three year follow-up using questionnaires. The OS Subcommittee—made up of selected NIH and Vanguard Clinical Center investigators—suggested many variables, most of which were then included in the CT questionnaires.* The variables remaining in the supplemental questionnaire, which will be given only to OS participants, reflect more speculative issues than those addressed by the CT. However, although the WHI *Manual of Operations and Procedures* notes that "(t)he content of the supplemental questionnaire is directed to the epidemiology of primary outcomes that are relatively common, serious, and capable of being readily ascertained by means of the planned OS follow-up mechanisms" (1993), the committee was provided with little information about the possible specific etiologic associations and the additional hypotheses being studied in the OS.

DESIGN AND METHODS

The OS is designed as an observational prospective cohort study. Women who have been contacted and expressed interest in the CT, but who are ineligible or unwilling to participate, will be asked to participate in the OS. Being drawn from the same area and age group, the women in the OS and CT will be in some ways comparable and, as volunteers, are likely to be different from the population as a whole. The women in the OS are likely to differ from CT participants in other respects, including their health behavior, history, and status. The incidence rates of disease and the extent of exposure to risk factors may be different among the CT, OS, and the general populations.

Despite, the OS participants having been drawn from a "convenience" sample, not a population-based sample, the OS population will be useful for examining associations between possible risk factors and disease; there is no a priori reason to believe that associations between possible risk factors and diseases will be different in this subgroup.

In addition to the information obtained by questionnaires, a fasting blood draw (and in some cases a urine collection) will provide specimens to be frozen and stored. The May 1991 Repository Feasibility Study from the National Cancer Institute estimates that between 10 and 20 million samples will be stored for the entire CT and OS populations. Serum storage is potentially valuable because it is likely that over the next several years hypotheses concerned with biological markers of exposures or of early disease will be formulated outside of the WHI that can be examined in this study population. A 1 percent subsample stratified on age, racial/ethnic group, and socioeconomic status will have repeat baseline information after the first screening visit so that the reliability of the data can be determined and error correction methods applied. This reliability testing strengthens the study.

---

*Questionnaire categories include: Personal Information, Medical History, Reproductive History, Family History, Personal Habits, Psychosocial, Food Frequency, and OS Supplement.

All 100,000 OS participants will receive follow-up materials by mail at year one, and will be scheduled to return to the clinic for a follow-up visit at year three. Between 5 and 6 percent of the OS group will return to the clinic every three years for physical examination and laboratory measures; all 100,000 OS participants will be contacted annually by mail for follow-up. Bone densitometry studies and urine samples will be collected from the OS participants at the three osteoporosis substudy centers every three years. The Clinical Coordinating Center estimates the cost of the first year follow-up by mail and the year three follow-up visit to be $8.5 million.

The OS will have more power than the CT for testing associations in minority populations, since the OS anticipates enrolling 20,000 minority women. Investigators will attempt to recruit minority women to reflect their proportion in the general population of women aged 50-79 years in each clinical center region (approximately 17 percent of the population in the United States is nonwhite). Overall, anticipated OS enrollment by racial/ethnic subgroup is: African American: 10,000; Hispanic: 6,000; Native American: 2,000; Asian and Pacific Islanders: 2,000; and white: 80,000.

The committee feels that the elements of the analytic plan, as described by NIH, seem appropriate. Regression methods will be used to estimate relative risks. Nested case-control sampling can be used to reduce the number of blood specimens that will need to be analyzed for hypotheses concerned with serum. In instances in which measurements are stable over time, case-cohort sampling can be used.

COST

Including the OS as a WHI component is inexpensive relative to a free-standing observational trial of this size, because the infrastructure to support the study would already be in place. For example, the same number of women need to be contacted initially for the CT regardless of whether they are retained for the OS. NIH is unable to distinguish the overall costs of the OS from the costs of the CT because both components were generated simultaneously. The only available estimate of OS costs comes from the Clinical Coordinating Center. It estimates the marginal costs of the OS (i.e., those costs over and above the cost of the CT, which includes the vast identification, recruitment, and screening process) to be approximately $10,570,000, that is, $105 per person over the planned 12-year duration of the OS recruitment and follow-up period. If accurate, that is a good cost per person; if it is a low estimate, the actual cost could still be reasonable.

Although data collection is included in the WHI cost estimate, many costs of analysis and publication are not considered. When additional funds are sought for analysis, both the cost and the scientific yield of the OS will increase.

RECOMMENDATIONS

The committee agrees with NIH that the OS is potentially a rich source of data within the WHI at a reasonable cost. However, the committee is concerned that it was not provided with historical material explaining the additional hypotheses being tested in the OS (beyond the DM, HRT, and CaD supplementation hypotheses). It is unclear whether the lack of such material reflects the prudent concentration of NIH staff on the CT when collecting material for the committee or a true lack of recent attention to the additional hypotheses being tested.

- **The committee recommends that NIH treat the OS as a precious investment even though its cost relative to the entire WHI is low. The progress of the OS should be monitored carefully to ensure that the quality of the data is as high as possible, losses to follow-up are minimized, and carefully framed investigations are pursued.**

- The committee also strongly recommends that NIH make the OS data available to qualified investigators outside the WHI network early enough to maximize the use of the data. Outside investigators should be able to add ancillary studies to the OS. Such data availability will increase the scientific and public health yield of this public investment, increasing the justification of the expenditure. Clear policies about the timing and conditions under which the data and cohort will be made available to outside investigators need to be established from the outset.

- The committee's recommendation for the CT Objective Prescheduled Reassessment, outlined in Chapter 2, has implications for the OS. For example, if the CT should end after eight years, the coordination and funding of the OS would be significantly affected. The committee encourages NIH and the WHI OS Subcommittee to consider these possibilities and devise contingency plans for the OS.

4

Community Prevention Study

INTRODUCTION

NIH has not provided a clear vision for the Community Prevention Study (CPS). The hypotheses for this component of the Women's Health Initiative (WHI) are less specific than those of the Clinical Trial (CT); the rationale, design, and methods are incompletely described. Only an initial plan for the CPS has been presented thus far, and consequently the committee is unsure of the scope of the CPS or the resources necessary to complete it. Nevertheless, the committee is supportive of the concept presented in the 1992 WHI Concept Review Document to develop practical community-based strategies needed to achieve many national goals for women's health.

NIH representatives discussed plans for the CPS during the committee's June 1993 meeting, but no firm plans or cost estimate were provided. The committee estimates that between $25 and $50 million of the funds allocated for the WHI may be available to fund the CPS. This was calculated by subtracting the current cost estimates of the CT and OS from the total available WHI monies of $625 million. In considering the tremendous need for strategies that would result in lifestyle change in women, particularly among lower socioeconomic status (SES) and minority women, the committee feels that an amount as low as $25 million will not suffice.

RATIONALE

The WHI Concept Review Document pertaining to the Community Prevention Studies (March 9, 1992) states that there are two major purposes for the WHI. The CT is designed to test hypotheses, and the OS is designed to either generate or support hypotheses, but neither is designed to develop methods for implementing the recommendations that might ensue from the trials. These implementation methodologies are to be the province of the third major component of the WHI: the community study. Originally termed the Community Randomized Trial (CRT), this trial was reconceptualized in June 1993 and is now called the Community Prevention Study (CPS). The CPS is currently under development; a consultant's meeting was held on July 19, 1993, and a concept review meeting is scheduled for later in 1993.

The rationale that distinguished the CRT, as originally designed, from the CT was the "second major purpose" of the WHI: "to evaluate strategies to achieve healthful behaviors including improved diet, smoking prevention and cessation, increased physical activity, and early disease detection, for women of diverse ethnic groups and socioeconomic strata." The description of the CRT makes it clear that the study was designed to address the broad social and political context of the risk factors under examination. These activities were have to been consistent with the health promotion and disease prevention objectives of *Healthy People 2000*, with a practical emphasis on the dearth of strategies to achieve those objectives. Furthermore, the CRT planners identified the prior successes of comprehensive community-based programs and the diverse strategies that communities implement as a further rationale for the trial. The original CRT design involved a multicenter field trial in which 16 pairs of communities would be randomized to a set of community interventions. The target age group was women over 40, and sample sizes and power calculations were based on an assumed five years of intervention. Interventions were to be directed at smoking prevention and cessation, dietary pattern, physical activity, and early disease detection for cervical and breast cancer. The CRT's goal, in addition to "promoting a lifestyle of healthful behavior in women 40 and older," was to establish and reinforce the infrastructure through which to promote women's health so that the infrastructure would remain at a functioning level following study completion.

The rationale of the redesigned community study, now called the Community Prevention Study (CPS), appears to be similar to the CRT with respect to developing strategies to change the risk factors and health habits relevant to various major chronic diseases of women. This objective is to be achieved, according to NIH, by a series of Requests for Applications. The CPS differs from the CRT in its emphasis on encouraging study of strategies that need development before they are suitable for universal use in multiple communities. The CPS emphasizes the existence of major gaps in diet, exercise, and smoking change programs for women in general, and especially for low-SES and ethnic minority women. This change in rationale rests in part on a changed belief within NIH that a formal randomized trial in 32 communities (the original plan) was premature, and that methods to achieve change in various components of a broad multifactor community trial needed development before they were placed in a formal randomized design.

DESIGN AND METHODS

The rather sketchy June 1993 design of the CPS suggests a similarity to its CRT predecessor in its language regarding the overall method of community intervention. It differs in its call for pilot studies to evaluate the methodology and feasibility of these interventions.

Although the methodology for the project has not yet been formally defined, the Committee has several suggestions:

- Project selection should ensure that components are suitable for incorporation into comprehensive community-based programs.
- Projects should attempt to decrease unfavorable disparities between lower SES and racial/ethnic minority women and higher SES non-minority women and to promote the creation of culturally appropriate strategies at low cost.
- Projects should include strong training components (which will permit personnel to train others in additional communities), possibly resulting in a set of regional training centers.
- Projects should employ many process measures needed for cost-effectiveness analyses.
- Projects that are multifactor in both risk factors and targeted methods of intervention should be favored.

In addition, projects should include attention to regulatory and environmental changes when feasible; however, more limited and often single-factor projects may provide useful information yet be lacking in the environmental or regulatory change dimension. The CPS should also emphasize projects that promote the creation of culturally appropriate strategies at low cost. Comparisons among strategies can yield much needed data on cost-effectiveness.

COST

If the CPS is to encompass geographic differences, ethnic minority needs, needs related to SES, many health topics and risk factors, and a variety of strategies to address all of these issues, then a reasonably large number of projects would be necessary. A matrix of target groups, risk factors, and strategies would easily justify 50 projects. As mentioned in the CT cost section in Chapter 2, if additional Clinical Centers are funded at $8 or $9 million each, approximately $570 to $580 million of the $625 million total has been committed for the CT and OS before consideration of funding the CPS (a total remainder of only $45-55 million). However, if the additional Clinical Centers is more expensive than expected, and the total funding necessary for the CT and OS is $600 million, an even lower $25 million would be reserved for the CPS.

RECOMMENDATIONS

The committee endorses the general plans described to date for the CPS, and NIH is to be commended for creating the concept of multiple RFAs under a cooperative agreement. This will allow the development of the many strategies for change that are needed to fill the gaps in women's health, particularly those that relate to low-SES and minority women. These strategies are needed to achieve various lifestyle changes and the goals of *Healthy People 2000*; thus, the CPS is separate from and complementary to the CT. The committee therefore makes the following recommendation:

- **The development of the Community Prevention Study should be equal importance with the CT and OS.** The committee recommends that NIH consider it a matter of some urgency to develop a more definitive plan for the CPS. The level of resources allocated for the CPS should be an affirmative decision, one that is based on the appropriate funding necessary to accomplish the task, not one obtained through what might be left over from the other two components of the WHI.

The committee also feels that certain aspects of the CPS are critical to highlight, and urges the NIH to seriously consider the following suggestions:

- *Given the importance of women's health and the vast range of circumstances influencing it, fund numerous projects (probably between 40 and 50) over approximately eight years.* These projects should adequately encompass needs related to diversity of health topic; intended recipients of interventions; geographic regions of varied cultures; and approach or strategy. Within the eight-year project, three years of funding is recommended in order to focus on strengthening infrastructure development and dissemination techniques.

- *Target approximately $50 to $100 million for the CPS.*

- *Develop NIH internal resources in conjunction with the coordinating and disseminating functions related to the CPS.* In general, NIH should strengthen its public health and disease prevention component; the coordination and dissemination activities of the CPS can aid NIH in reaching that goal.

- *Ensure that a mechanism (such as comparable data collection instruments) exists to link the projects and facilitate useful exchanges among investigators.* This would also serve to transfer knowledge and technology to relevant communities during a later dissemination phase. The cooperative agreement is considered as a possible mechanism for this purpose.

5

Concluding Remarks

The three preceding chapters discuss the committee's findings about and recommendations for each component of the Women's Health Initiative (WHI). In this chapter the committee would like to address the WHI as a whole by reflecting upon the questions posed in the IOM Statement of Task, as well as interconnected concerns that relate both to the societal context of the WHI as well as to the IOM committee assessment.

RESPONSE TO THE STATEMENT OF TASK

1. What was the rationale behind the choice of these particular studies? Are appropriate topics considered? Should other topics be included?

NIH has provided a justifiable rationale for the diseases selected for study in the WHI. These diseases are important causes of morbidity and mortality among women in the United States; they merit further research to test the efficacy of preventive measures and to develop effective programs that educate and motivate women to adopt proven prevention strategies. Heart disease and cancer are the leading causes of death among women, and the high incidence of breast cancer is appropriately a matter of concern. Osteoporotic fractures, which occur with much higher frequency among women than men, are a leading cause of disability among older women. Research leading to prevention of these conditions, or at least postponement of the age of onset, would be expected to improve substantially the quality of life of older women.

NIH could have chosen other diseases or risk factors for ill health as the focus for the WHI, and those choices could also be defended. There are many unanswered questions regarding prevention of illness, enhancement of well-being, and delay of morbidity and mortality while maintaining an acceptable quality of life.

Because the WHI is among the most complex studies ever undertaken, and because the WHI Clinical Trial (CT) is already under way, it would not be appropriate to suggest other topics to be included. This might overburden an already complex set of studies, could incur additional costs, and would almost certainly lead to further delays. Moreover, as noted above, it was not the committee's task to redesign the WHI.

2. Are the methodologies and the study designs appropriate to address the stated research objectives? Is the size of the study population appropriate?

The methodologies selected—a clinical trial, an observational study, and community studies—are appropriate for the study of the efficacy or effectiveness of certain interventions to improve women's health, for generating further hypotheses, and for implementing and evaluating community intervention strategies. Because details of the Community Prevention Study (CPS) have not been decided, little can be said about the appropriateness of the specific methods and designs of the study. The majority of NIH staff time and effort has been devoted to designing the CT; therefore, it is the focus of most of the comments and recommendations in this report.

Three primary hypotheses are the basis of the CT:

- A low fat dietary pattern will reduce the incidence of breast cancer and colorectal cancer;
- Hormone replacement therapy will reduce the incidence of cardiovascular disease; and
- Calcium and vitamin D supplements will reduce the incidence of osteoporotic hip fracture.

The design of the trial, the number of women who will participate, and the methods used to determine health status all flow from these hypotheses. Some of the design decisions are based on evidence obtained from earlier studies, and some decisions are based on assumptions. Assumptions must be made regarding many aspects of any clinical trial, and examples include the strength of the protective effect, the number and timing of the endpoint events (occurrence of heart attacks, hip fractures, breast cancer), the ability to recruit and retain the study participants, and the ability to maintain adherence and behavior change in the intervention groups.

To determine whether the proposed methods for the CT were appropriate for the stated research objectives, the committee analyzed the assumptions underlying the methods for each hypothesis and identified the major threats to the successful achievement of each hypothesis. The committee then weighed the risks of an unsuccessful trial against the potential benefits of additional information to be learned from a successful trial.

Using this approach, the primary hypothesis that a low fat dietary pattern will reduce breast cancer and colorectal cancer incidence was judged by the committee to be inappropriate for emphasis as a primary hypothesis in the trial. The primary hypotheses of the HRT branch and the CaD branches were judged to be appropriate.

Several secondary hypotheses are also included in the design of the CT. Most prominent is the hypothesis that a low fat dietary pattern will reduce the incidence of cardiovascular disease. Using the same approach of weighing the threats of an unsuccessful

CONCLUDING REMARKS 87

trial against the benefits of a successful trial, the committee judged this secondary hypothesis to be appropriate for inclusion as a primary hypothesis in the trial.

These conclusions led to specific recommendations about the design and conduct of the CT, which are presented in chapter 2.

3. Are the costs accurately estimated and sufficient to reach the desired objectives?

Cost estimates are fairly well developed for the CT, deducible for the Observational Study (OS), and absent for the CPS. To a large extent, this reflects the stage of development of each component. It is therefore difficult to say with certainty that overall costs are sufficient to reach the objectives of the WHI.

The CT appears to be very tightly budgeted. Although the approximately $1,000 per participant per year costs are within the range of costs (unadjusted for inflation) NIH incurred for other clinical trials conducted over the past 20 years, they are very low relative to the costs of more recently conducted comparable trials.

As noted earlier, the committee believes that the total costs of the CT will be greater than the $625 million provided by NIH. NIH and Vanguard Center representatives have indicated that the additional funds necessary for successful completion of the trial will be covered by the institutions in which the Vanguard Centers are based. This reliance on institutional support may be reasonable in the case of the Vanguard Centers, but the committee felt it is unlikely that an additional 29 institutions can be identified that have both the experience to carry out the tasks of high quality research and the ability to provide additional resources. If all participating institutions honor their agreements to provide additional support for the CT, and if there are no unanticipated problems, the budgeted amount might be sufficient. However, it is very unlikely that there will be no problems.

4. Will the study produce sufficiently reliable results to justify the costs?

The committee concluded that valuable scientific information could be obtained in the redesigned study. However, the question of whether the investment is justified is, in part, a question about cost-effectiveness, and that involves consideration of alternative study designs. The committee thought it likely that much of the information could be obtained in better designed, smaller, more focused studies that could have a greater chance of success and probably be less costly. However, it recognized that a study in a broad-based population can have merit and proponents as well. The committee did not consider its task to be a consideration of alternative designs, and did not do so. Thus, the committee admits some skepticism about the merits of this particular investment, but it cannot offer a definitive conclusion about cost-effectiveness.

It is important to note that the modified study that the committee felt could be justified scientifically is quite different in its aims from the study proposed by NIH. The study proposed by NIH has as a primary focus the test of whether DM will reduce the risk of breast cancer. The modified study focuses on CHD. If NIH decides to accept the recommendations of the committee about modification of the study, it will need to consider whether the methods and study population proposed to test interventions on the risk of both CHD and breast cancer should be the same as those for a test of effects on the risk of CHD. Moreover, NIH will need to consider whether the study objectives that can be achieved in the modified study are worth the investment.

Whatever the merits of the WHI, the committee has no doubt about the need for a substantial investment in research on women's health.

SOCIETAL CONTEXT

The committee contemplated the societal context of the WHI throughout its more focused discussions of study rationale, design and methods, and cost, specifically the following issues:

- efficacy and effectiveness,
- public health choice versus individual choice, and
- considerations beyond science.

Efficacy and Effectiveness

In assessing whether a study is successful, one looks at whether it added more evidence toward answering a question. Obviously, whether the question is posed appropriately affects this assessment. It is not clear to the committee whether the WHI CT is designed as a test of efficacy or a test of effectiveness. And therein lies much of the difficulty in interpreting criticism of the CT.

Framed as a test of the efficacy of a low fat dietary pattern in reducing the incidence of coronary heart disease, for example, the CT will be plagued from the start. If there is no difference in coronary heart disease incidence between intervention and control groups, does one conclude—as an efficacy trial is set up to do—that the intervention is not associated with a change in outcome? Or might one state that, *as followed*, the dietary intervention did not have an effect? To be able to state the efficacy finding with assurance, one would need evidence that the dietary intervention in fact took place. Yet, as critics have pointed out, there is no available biomarker for fat intake and state-of-the-art measures of food intake are inexact, depending on respondent memory, honesty, and ability to report what they have eaten.

Similar questions exist with the hormone replacement intervention. Is the HRT branch testing whether 0.625 mg of conjugated equine estrogen daily, with or without 2.5 mg of medroxyprogesterone, affects the risks of cardiovascular disease, osteoporotic fractures, and breast and endometrial cancers? Or is it testing whether the availability of HRT, with all of its perceived and actual side effects, and the related achieved adherence, are related to the measured outcomes?

NIH officials seem unsure of whether the CT, at this point in its development, is a test of efficacy or effectiveness. The committee suggests that it is somewhere in between. Given the extensive, though imperfect, data collection over the course of the study, it is possible that investigators will be able to acquire some information on efficacy, but it is less likely that they will acquire enough information to answer the basic question. The CT will be more likely to assess whether efforts to make major lifestyle and drug interventions (HRT and DM) are *effective* in changing certain risks of morbidity and mortality.

That test of effectiveness is still of major public health importance, but the committee reiterates a point it made earlier: no one study is sufficient. Other, smaller studies must explore the biological and behavioral intricacies of each larger lifestyle intervention, in order to determine which elements are efficacious and why. Then, additional studies on the effectiveness of lifestyle interventions must develop methods generalizable beyond clinical trial volunteers. The committee assumes that NIH would continue to fund such a range of studies as part of its overall research agenda.

Public Health Choice Versus Individual Choice

Individuals want to be able to make choices. Some choose to let their doctors choose; others want more personal control. For some people, length of life is most important; for others, quality is the determining factor. For most, it is an unenunciated, ill-defined combination.

Meanwhile, NIH faces a dilemma. It seeks to examine multiple endpoints but needs to make a binary decision—to stop or continue the trial. How can it resolve that dilemma? Total mortality is a useful initial methodologic approach, as well as a useful public health endpoint. It will inform some decisions that must be made for a community as a whole. Total mortality is not sufficient, however, for public health decisions or individual decisions about health care. Total mortality includes increased mortality from some diseases and decreased mortality from others. It ignores increased or decreased disabilities, pain, deformity, ease of life—in sum, the quality of life. It may also mask increased risk for some subgroups. Individuals, having different levels of comfortable risk-taking, fears, desires, and personal circumstances, might make different choices for themselves than a well-meaning government or science council might for the group as a whole. Thus, whatever the outcome of the CT, choices for individual women need to be informed by their own baseline risk, fears of adverse outcomes, desire for potential benefits, and willingness to seek alternatives.

Considerations Beyond Science

The committee's charge was to examine the meaningfulness of potential results from the WHI in terms of rationale, study design and methods, cost, and overall justification. However, the committee was constantly faced with broader considerations. Colleagues, advocacy organizations, executive and legislative branch representatives, all approached the committee with reasons why the WHI should proceed, and why canceling it would unleash disasters. If it is cancelled, some argued, no one would ever trust the government again; it would prove that the government does not really care about women's health; it would so greatly disappoint the community which has gathered around this project that it will be impossible to ever galvanize them again; it would be seen as an unwelcome political blow to those in Congress who have pressed for more women's health research.

Others argued that it would be wrong and harmful to women's health to spend $625 million and find after 14 years that little in the way of useful information had been learned. It would not help women's health and women's health research to publicly announce and then misuse an enormous amount of money.

The committee tried to keep these considerations out of its judgment on the merits of the science, but they are important issues. With the committee recommendation that the WHI could proceed—though with significant changes of duration and focus—the discussion of these issues should continue.

References

Barrett-Connor E, Kritz-Silverstein D. Estrogen replacement therapy and cognitive function in older women. *Journal of the American Medical Association* 269:2637-41, 1993.

Bush TL, Cowan LD, Barrett-Connor E, Criqui MH, Karon JM, Wallace RB, Tyroler HA, Rifkind BM. Estrogen use and all-cause mortality. Preliminary results from the Lipid Research Clinics Program follow-up study. *Journal of the American Medical Association* 249:903-6, 1983.

Christiansen C. Hormone replacement therapy for established osteoporosis in elderly women. *Clinical Obstetrics and Gynaecology* 5:853-6, 1991.

Devor M, Barrett-Connor E, Renvall M, Feigal D, Ramsdell J. Estrogen replacement therapy and the risk of venous thrombosis. *American Journal of Medicine* 92:275-82, 1992.

Henderson MM, Kushi LH, Thompson DJ, Gorbach SL, Clifford CK, Insull W, Moskowitz M, Thompson RS. Feasibility of a randomized trial of a low-fat diet for the prevention of breast cancer: Dietary compliance in the Women's Health Trial Vanguard Study. *Preventive Medicine* 19:115-133, 1990.

Howe GR, Hirohata T, Hislop TG, Iscovich JM, Yuan J-M, Katsouyanni K, Lubin F, Marubini E, Modan B, Rohan T, Toniolo P, Shunzhang Y. Dietary factors and risk of breast cancer: Combined analysis of 12 case-control studies. *Journal of the National Cancer Institute* 82(7):561-569, 1990.

Howe GR, Benito E, Castelleto R, Cornee J, Esteve J, Gallagher RP, Iscovich JM, Deng-ao J, Kaaks R, Kune GA, Kune S, L'Abbe KA, Lee HP, Lee M, Miller AB, Peters RK, Potter JD, Riboli E, Slattery ML, Trichopoulos D, Tuyns A, Tzonou A, Whittemore AS, Wu-Williams AH, Shu Z. Dietary intake of fiber and decreased risk of cancers of the colon and rectum: Evidence from the combined analysis of 13 case-control studies. *Journal of the National Cancer Institute* 84(24):1887-1896, 1992.

Lakatos E. Sample sizes based on the log-rank statistic in complex clinical trials. *Biometrics* 44:229-241, 1988.

National Cancer Institute. Repository Feasibility Study. May 1991.

Potter JD, Slattery ML, Bostick RM, Gapstur SM. Colon cancer: A review of the epidemiology. Forthcoming in *Epidemiological Reviews* 15(2), 1993.

Prentice RL, Kakar F, Hursting S, Sheppard L, Klein R, Kushi LH. Aspects of the rationale for the Women's Health Trial. *Journal of the National Cancer Institute* 80(11):802-814, 1988.

Prentice RL. Aspects of the science of cancer prevention trials: Lessons from the conduct and planning of clinical trials of a low-fat diet intervention among women. *Preventive Medicine* 20:147-157, 1991.

Prentice RL. Letter to Dr. Susan Thaul. July 8, 1993. Attachments.

Quigley MET, Martin PL, Burnier AM, Brooks P. Estrogen therapy arrests bone loss in elderly women. *American Journal of Obstetrics and Gynecology* 156:1516-23, 1987.

Self S, Prentice R, Iverson D, Henderson M, Thompson D, Byar D, Insull W, Gorbach SL, Clifford C, Goldman S, Urban N, Sheppard L, Greenwald P. Statistical design of the Women's Health Trial. *Controlled Clinical Trials* 9:119-136, 1988.

Stampfer MJ, Colditz GA. Estrogen replacement therapy and coronary heart disease: a quantitative assessment of the epidemiologic evidence. *Preventive Medicine* 20:47-63, 1991.

Stangel JJ, Innerfield I, Reyniak JV, Stone ML. The effect of conjugated estrogens on coagulability in menopausal women. *Obstetrics and Gynecology* 49:314-16, 1977.

United States House of Representatives' Appropriations Committee Report 102-708. July 23, 1992.

Wilson PWF. Postmenopausal estrogen use, cigarette smoking, and cardiovascular morbidity in women over 50: The Framingham Study. *New England Journal of Medicine* 313:1038-43, 1985.

Women's Health Initiative. Community Prevention Studies Description. June 1993.

Women's Health Initiative. Concept Review Document on the Community Prevention Study. March 9, 1992.

Women's Health Initiative. Concept Review Document on the Clinical Trial and the Observational Studies. March 9, 1992.

Women's Health Initiative. Manual of Operations and Procedures, Volume 2. Draft, May 1993.

REFERENCES

Women's Health Initiative. Protocol. June 28, 1993.

Wren BG. The effect of oestrogen on the female cardiovascular system. *Medical Journal of Australia* 157:204-8, 1992.

Appendixes

A

Clinical Trial Exclusion Criteria
(June 28, 1993, WHI Protocol)

A. Exclusion Criteria for All Components

1. Competing Risk: Any medical condition associated with predicted survival of less than three years in the judgment of a Clinic physician (e.g., class IV congestive heart failure, obstructive lung disease requiring long-term ventilation or supplemental oxygen in the past, severe chronic liver disease with jaundice or ascites, kidney failure requiring dialysis, sickle cell anemia)

2. Adherence or Retention Reasons

   - alcoholism
   - other drug dependency
   - mental illness, including severe depression
   - dementia
   - active participant in any other intervention trial where participants are individually randomized to an intervention or control group

B. Additional Exclusion Criteria for All Clinical Trial Components

1. Competing Risk

   - invasive cancer of any type in the past 10 years
   - breast cancer at any time (in situ or invasive)
   - any medical condition associated with predicted survival of less than five years in the judgment of a Clinic physician (e.g., class IV congestive heart failure, obstructive lung disease requiring long-term ventilation or supplemental oxygen in the past, severe chronic liver disease with jaundice or ascites, kidney failure requiring dialysis, sickle cell anemia)

SOURCE: Adapted from National Institute of Health's WHI Protocol, June 28, 1993, p.28.

- baseline mammogram or clinical breast examination findings suspicious of breast cancer (see MOOP for detailed criteria)*
- acute myocardial infarction in past six months*
- stroke or transient ischemic attack (TIA) within the past six months*
- known chronic active hepatitis or severe cirrhosis

2. Safety reasons

- severely underweight (BMI < 18 kg/m² or loss of 15 or more pounds in previous six months)
- hematocrit < 34% or hemoglobin < 11.5 gm/dl*
- platelets < 75,000 cells/ml
- severe hypertension (systolic BP > 200 mmHg or diastolic BP > 105 mmHg)*
- current use of oral daily corticosteroids for more than six months

3. Adherence or retention reasons

- BMI > 40 kg/m²
- unwilling to participate in baseline or yearly examination components such as yearly mammograms, clinical breast exams, phlebotomy, electrocardiograms, questionnaires and forms; or unable to complete baseline study requirements

C. **Additional Exclusion Criteria for Hormone Replacement Component**

1. Safety reasons

- endometrial cancer of any stage at any time
- endometrial hyperplasia at baseline biopsy or endometrial thickness > 5mm via ultrasonography (no recycling)
- malignant melanoma of any stage at any time
- non-traumatic thromboembolic event or thromboembolic event associated with estrogen or oral contraceptive use
- previous osteoporosis-related fracture being treated with hormone replacement therapy
- history of bleeding disorder serious enough to require transfusion
- known history of hypertriglyceridemia, or lipemic serum leading to diagnosis of hypertriglyceridemia on baseline blood draw
- deep vein thrombosis or pulmonary embolism in past six months*
- currently on anticoagulants*
- currently on tamoxifen

---

* Implies that a woman who is temporarily excluded may be reevaluated for eligibility as appropriate to the excluding condition. If more than six months have elapsed since the woman's first screening visit, however, all baseline and screening activities must be repeated.

2. Adherence or retention reasons

- severe menopausal symptoms that would make placebo therapy intolerable to the participant
- inadequate adherence with placebo run-in (less than 80% of pills taken)
- unable or unwilling to discontinue use of hormone replacement therapy (women must discontinue current replacement hormone therapy for at least three months in order to be eligible for the HRT)*
- unwilling to have baseline or yearly endometrial aspirations*

D. Additional Exclusion Criteria for Dietary Modification Component

1. Adherence or retention reasons

- special dietary requirements incompatible with the intervention diet (such as celiac sprue, other malabsorption syndromes, use of MAO inhibitors). Women will be eligible if they are following a diabetic diet or a low salt diet
- colorectal cancer at any time
- unable to complete Four-Day Food Record adequately
- percent of calories from fat estimated to be 34 or less
- number of main meals prepared out of home $\geq$ 10 per week
- type I (insulin-requiring, ketosis-prone) diabetes mellitus
- gastrointestinal conditions that contraindicate a high fiber diet

E. Additional Exclusion Criteria for Calcium/Vitamin D Component

1. Safety reasons

- History of renal calculi

2. Adherence or retention reasons

- unable or unwilling to discontinue use of calcium or vitamin D supplements
- inadequate adherence with HRT and/or DM trial components during the first year of followup (see Manual of Operations and Procedures for detailed criteria)

B

U.S. House of Representatives Appropriations Committee

102D CONGRESS		REPORT
2d Session	HOUSE OF REPRESENTATIVES	102-708

DEPARTMENTS OF LABOR, HEALTH AND HUMAN SERVICES, AND EDUCATION, AND RELATED AGENCIES APPROPRIATION BILL, 1993

JULY 23, 1992.—Committed to the Committee of the Whole House on the State of the Union and ordered to be printed

Mr. NATCHER, from the Committee on Appropriations,
submitted the following

REPORT

[To accompany H.R. 5677]

The Committee on Appropriations submits the following report in explanation of the accompanying bill making appropriations for the Departments of Labor, Health and Human Services (except the Food and Drug Administration, Indian Health Service, and the Office of Consumer Affairs), and Education (except Indian Education), Action, the Corporation for Public Broadcasting, the Federal Mediation and Conciliation Service, the Federal Mine Safety and Health Review Commission, the National Commission on Acquired Immune Deficiency Syndrome, the National Commission on Libraries and Information Science, the National Commission on Responsibilities for Financing Postsecondary Education, the National Council on Disability, the National Labor Relations Board, the National Mediation Board, the Occupational Safety and Health Review Commission, the Prospective Payment Assessment Commission, the Physician Payment Review Commission, ...

Women's Health Initiative.—The Women's Health Initiative, a trans-NIH project, was designed to study the major causes of death, disability and frailty in post-menopausal women. The project has three parts: a clinical trial that will investigate new strategies to prevent cancer, cardiovascular disease and osteoporosis; an observational component that will explore new causative factors for these conditions; and a community trial that will test the application of preventive approaches targeting behaviors identified in the "Healthy People 2000" report. It is estimated that three years will be required to recruit project participants and that nine years of follow-up will be needed to determine the benefits and risks of preventive interventions.

The Committee is concerned by testimony of the Director of NIH that the life-cycle cost estimate for the Women's Health Initiative has increased from $500 million to $619 million. While the Committee has provided $43 million for the 1993 cost of this trial, it believes that the study design and cost estimates should be thoroughly reviewed by an external group with expertise in this area. The NIH is directed to contract with the Institute of Medicine for such a review, which should be completed not later than February 1, 1993. This study should focus on the issue of cost, as well as the issue of whether the study will produce sufficiently reliable results to justify such a massive investment. The cost of this review, estimated at $250,000, should be financed as quickly as possible after this report is issued by reallocating funds within the 1992 allocation for the women's initiative. The Committee understands that the Director may wish to fund other reviews of this type as well as the Institute of Medicine study and has no objection to additional evaluations of such an expensive undertaking.

Minority Health Initiative.—The Minority Health Initiative (MHI) is another major trans-NIH project with the objectives of closing existing minority health gaps . . . .

Source: From House Report 102-708, pages 1 and 90.

C

Statement of Task

The committee will review the design, organization, and operation plans of the Women's Health Initiative (WHI) to answer, at the end of a six-month period, the following questions:

1. What was the rationale behind the choice of these particular studies? Are appropriate topics considered? Should other topics be included?
2. Are the methodologies and the study designs appropriate to address the stated research objectives? Is the size of the study population appropriate?
3. Are the costs accurately estimated and sufficient to reach the desired objectives?
4. Will the study produce sufficiently reliable results to justify the costs?

To support the review and recommendation deliberations, the committee will:

1. Review documents provided by the National Institutes of Health (NIH), including the Requests for Proposals (RFPs), responses to the RFPs by the entities awarded contracts as the Clinical Coordinating Center and the fifteen Vanguard Clinical Centers, and public testimony concerning the NIH plan;
2. Conduct critical review of published literature appropriate for the fields of study; and
3. Seek the counsel of recognized experts in the intervention and outcome fields of study, as well as experts in the estimation and management of cost, by way of workshops conducted concurrently with the committee meetings.

The Committee will meet three times over the six-month study period. The Committee will invite NIH scientists involved in the WHI design and investigators from the funded Coordinating Center and the Vanguard Centers to participate in workshops coincident with the first two meetings.

A final report will be delivered to the sponsor at the end of the study, with an interim copy of the final report to be delivered 14 days before public release of the report.

D

Documents Received by the Institute of Medicine from the National Institutes of Health

Received: March 1993
- Solicitation (RFP) NIH-WH-92-13
  Clinical Coordinating Center for the Clinical Trials and Observational
  Dated: 3/1/72
- Amendments to Solicitation NIH-WH-92-13
  Clinical Coordinating Center for the Clinical Trials and Observational
  Study of the Women's Health Initiative
  Dated: 4/22/92
- Solicitation (RFP) NIH-WH-92-19-E
  Vanguard Clinical Centers for Clinical Trials and Observational Study
  of the Women's Health Initiative
  Dated 4/29/92
- Amendments to Solicitation NIH-WH-92-19-E
  Vanguard Clinical Centers for Clinical Trials and Observational Study
  of the Women's Health Initiative
  Dated 4/29/92
- Information to Offerors
  Subheadings
    Scientific Information
    Objectives
    Inclusion Criteria for Clinical Trial
    Exclusion Criteria for Clinical Trial
    Enrollment
    Key Baseline and Follow-Up Variables
    Clinical Outcomes of Interest
  Partial Factorial Design
- Testimony from NIH Women's Health Initiative Public Hearing, October 28-29, 1991.

Received: May 25, 1993
- May 13, 1993 Protocol (was not yet approved)

Received: May 31, 1993
- March 8, 1993 Protocol (approved)

Received: July 7, 1993
Response to June 29, 1993 Dr. Thaul letter
- RFP: NIH-WH-93-30
- Business Proposals from the Vanguard Centers, with all cost information deleted
- June 28, 1993 Protocol (approved by the Data Safety and Monitoring Board, June 16, 1993) red-lined

Received: July 9, 1993
- Behavioral constructs
- Description and cost information of NIH-sponsored women's health studies

Received: July 12, 1993
Additional response to June 29, 1993 Dr. Thaul letter
- RFP: July 7, 1993
- Power calculations and sample size information from Laurence Freedman
- Additional quality of life construct information from Robert Kaplan
- Journal articles on clinical trials
- Incidence tables on colorectal cancer, hip fractures, and other fractures

Received: July 26, 1993
Additional response to June 29, 1993 Dr. Thaul letter
- VCC levels of effort and budget information (does not include salaries)
- Description and cost information of NHLBI-sponsored women's health studies
- Information and costs re Women's Health Studies in NIH institutes
- Proceedings from the October 28, 1991 Public Hearing
- Letter from Reubin Andres on the Baltimore Longitudinal Study
- Report on Progress: Study Design and Time Line. Memo, October 17, 1991.

Received: August 3, 1993
- Information on the Women's Health Trial Feasibility Study in Minority Populations
- May 13, 1991 Technical and Scientific Working Group, including:
    - Draft Proposal from NHLBI; Osteoporosis Component;
    - Draft Proposal from NCI and NHLBI;
    - Recommendations for Design of Trials;
    - NCI Biometry Branch; Recommendations for Cancer
    - Biomarker and Prevention Studies, NCI; and

- NCI Biometry Branch; Recommendations for Cancer
- Biomarker and Prevention Studies, NCI; and
- Repository Feasibility Information, NCI
- NIDDK Proposal for Obesity Component (May 13, 1991)
- Proposal by Scientific and Technical Working Group on WHI (June 4, 1991)
- Consultant Recommendations on Endometrial Biopsies (June 27, 1991)
- Reviews by Susan R. Johnson (On behalf of group of PEPI gynecology consultants) (July 23, 1991 and August 5, 1991)
- Minutes of Advisory Meeting on Calcium/Vitamin D Intervention (August 15, 1991)
- Minutes of Meeting with Expert Consultants in Epidemiology (September 13, 1991)
- Review by ICD Directors October 17, 1991
- Protocol Comments from Jeffrey A. Perlman, Chief, Contraceptive and Reproductive Evaluation Branch (October 22, 1991)
- Comments on WHI Prospectus by Linda J. Golden, FDA, Center for Drug Evaluation and Research (November 20, 1991)
- Minutes of Concept Review for Clinical Trial and Observational Study of the WHI (January 15, 1992)
- Minutes of Hormone Replacement Working Group Meeting (January 21, 1993)
- Minutes of Advisory Meeting for Dietary Intervention (May 10, 1993)

Received: August 4, 1993
Response to July 27, 1993 Dr. Thaul letter
- Memo from Jacques Rossouw, with attachments:
  - age distribution;
  - rate calculations;
  - power calculations;
  - discussion of dietary modification and breast cancer hypothesis;
  - Hollinghead scale;
  - adjustments to minority group rate;
  - budgets for additional 6,000 WHI CT participants;
  - subcommittee membership rosters;
  - Data Safety and Monitoring Board documents;
  - memo from Mark Kestin on plasma triglycerides and a low fat diet;
  - information on why calcium and vitamin D are combined in the Clinical Trial;
  - minutes from the Concept Review meeting for the Clinical Trial and Observational Study; and
  - the scripts for the VCC videotapes.

Additional response to June 29, 1993 Dr. Thaul letter
- Description and cost information of NIH-sponsored women's health studies, including:
  - NHLBI; NIDDK; NCI; NINDS; NCI; NIAMS; NIDR; NIAAA; NIA; and
  - other multi-ICD-sponsored studies

Received: August 11, 1993
- Information on conceivable changes in scope of work
- Information on WHI contract dates
- Additional description and cost information of NIH-sponsored women's health studies

E

Meeting Participants
June, July, and August 1993

Committee Members

Marion J. Finkel, M.D., *Chair*
Sandoz Pharmaceuticals Corporation

Lucile L. Adams-Campbell, Ph.D.
Howard University Cancer Center

Abdelmonem A. Afifi, Ph.D.
University of California, Los Angeles

Kelly D. Brownell, Ph.D.
Yale University

Gary R. Cutter, Ph.D.
Pythagoras, Inc.

John W. Farquhar, M.D.
Stanford University School of Medicine

M.R.C. Greenwood, Ph.D.
University of California, Davis
(Resigned July 7, 1993)

Jennifer L. Kelsey, Ph.D.
Stanford University School of Medicine

Penny M. Kris-Etherton, Ph.D., R.D.
The Pennsylvania State University

Joanne Lynn, M.D., M.A.
Dartmouth Medical School

Lynn Rosenberg, Sc.D.
Boston University School of Medicine

Diane B. Stoy, Ed.D., R.N.
The George Washington University
 Medical Center

Project Staff

Susan Thaul, Ph.D.
Study Director

Dana Hotra, M.H.S.
Research Associate

Donna Allen
Project Assistant

Felice LePar, B.A.
Research Assistant

IOM Staff

Queta Bond, Ph.D.
Executive Officer, IOM

Ruth E. Bulger, Ph.D.
Senior Program Officer
Health Sciences Policy Division

Joe Cassells, M.D.
Senior Program Officer
Health Sciences Policy Division

Valerie Setlow, Ph.D.
Director, Health Sciences Policy Division

Kenneth Shine, M.D.
President, IOM

Catherine E. Woteki, Ph.D., R.D.
Director, Food and Nutrition Board

Clinical Coordinating Center and Vanguard Center Representatives

William B. Applegate, M.D.
University of Tennessee-Memphis
  Prevention Center

Annlouise R. Assaf, Ph.D.
Memorial Hospital of Rhode Island
Division of Health Education

Gregory L. Burke, M.D., M.S.
The Bowman Gray
School of Medicine

Arlene Caggiula, Ph.D.
University of Pittsburgh
Graduate School of Public Health

Ralph Coates, Ph.D.
Emory University School of Medicine

Patricia Elmer, Ph.D., R.D.
University of Minnesota Medical School

Philip Greenland, M.D.
Northwestern University Medical School

Mary Haan, Ph.D., M.P.H.
University of California, Davis
School of Medicine

Maureen Henderson, M.D.
Fred Hutchinson Cancer
  Research Center

Robert D. Langer, M.D., M.P.H.
University of California, San Diego
School of Medicine

Norman L. Lasser, M.D.
University of Medicine and Dentistry
  of New Jersey

Kathryn Kalan, B.S.
Brigham and Women's Hospital, Boston

Lewis H. Kuller, M.D.
University of Pittsburgh
Graduate School of Public Health

Albert Oberman, M.D.
University of Alabama at Birmingham

Ross L. Prentice, Ph.D.
Clinical Coordinating Center
Fred Hutchinson Cancer
  Research Center

Douglas Taren, Ph.D.
University of Arizona

Robert Wallace, M.D.
University of Iowa

APPENDIX E

National Institutes of Health Officials

Susan Clark, M.A.
Project Officer

Caroline Clifford, Ph.D.
Chief, Diet and Cancer Branch
National Cancer Institute

Laurence Freedman, M.A.
Acting Chief, Biometry Branch
National Cancer Institute

Linda Gardner
Contracts Specialist

William Harlan, M.D.
Co-Director, Women's Health Initiative,
Associate Director, Office of
  Disease Prevention
Office of the Director

Carrie Hunter, M.D.
Special Assistant to the Director
Office of Research on Women's
  Health

Joan McGowan, Ph.D.
Chief, Bone Biology and Bone Diseases
Extramural Program
National Insitute of Arthritis and
  Musculoskeletal and Skin Diseases

Jacques Rossouw, M.D.
Project Officer
WHI Clinical Trial and
  Observational Study

Elaine Stone, Ph.D., M.P.H.
Health Scientist Administrator
Prevention and Demonstration
  Research Branch
National Heart Lung and Blood Institute

George Stone, Ph.D.
Grants Associate Program

Others

Mike Stephens, M.P.H.
U.S. House of Representatives
Appropriations Committee, Staff

Susan Wood, Ph.D.
Congressional Caucus on Women's
  Issues, Staff

F

Primary* and Subsidiary** Hypotheses of the Women's Health Initiative Clinical Trial

Dietary Modification Branch (DM):

* DM—in the form of a low-fat dietary pattern (reduced intake of total fat and saturated fat, increased intake of complex carbohydrate and fiber-containing foods)—will reduce the incidence of breast cancer and colorectal cancer, separately.
** DM will reduce the incidence of coronary heart disease.

Hormone Replacement Therapy Branch (HRT):

* Estrogen replacement therapy (ERT) and/or progestin and estrogen replacement therapy (PERT) will reduce the incidence of coronary heart disease and of other cardiovascular disease.
** ERT and/or PERT will reduce the incidence of all osteoporosis-related fractures and hip fractures, separately.
** ERT will increase the incidence of endometrial and breast cancer.
** PERT will increase the incidence of breast cancer.

Calcium and Vitamin D Supplementation Branch (CaD):

* CaD will reduce the incidence of hip fractures.
** CaD will reduce the incidence of colorectal cancer.

Subgroup Analyses

Some combinations of the treatments may have synergistic effects, while others may cancel out each other's effects. In addition, benefit or risk may also relate to some baseline

Source: Adapted from National Institute of Health's WHI Protocol, June 28, 1993, p. 28.

characteristic of the participants. The WHI will generally lack sufficient power to test these subgroup hypotheses unless there are unexpectedly large effects. However, subgroup analyses will be performed to examine:

- The effect of DM plus HRT on breast cancer incidence in women at high and low risk of breast cancer.
- The effect of DM plus HRT on the incidence of coronary and other cardiovascular disease and breast cancer, compared with each therapy alone.
- The effect of HRT on the incidence of coronary and other cardiovascular disease in women with and without cardiovascular disease at baseline.
- The effect of HRT on the incidence of coronary and other cardiovascular disease and breast cancer in obese and lean women.
- The effect of ERT on the incidence of coronary and other cardiovascular disease among women with and without a uterus.
- The effect of HRT plus CaD on fracture rates, compared with each therapy alone.
- The effect of CaD on fractures and colorectal cancer in women with lower and higher intakes of dietary calcium.
- The effect of DM, HRT, and CaD in subgroups of women defined by age and race/ethnicity.

Intermediate Variables

The CT will also offer an opportunity to examine a number of other pertinent factors, including the following:

- The effect of each treatment on perceived quality of life, on combined primary and secondary endpoints, and on total mortality.
- The effects of DM and HRT on lipids, lipoproteins, clotting factors, blood pressure, body mass index, waist-to-hip ratio, and blood glucose.
- Trends in the magnitude of DM, HRT, and CaD effects across age categories and across values of other participant characteristics.
- The relationship to clinical outcomes of (a) baseline biochemical and physical variables, (b) changes in those variables induced by treatment, and (c) adherence.
- The effect of the treatments on a variety of subsidiary endpoints, such as other cancers (ovarian, endometrial), diabetes mellitus, and other age-related outcomes.

G

Women's Health Initiative Committees

- Project Office within the Office of the NIH Director
- WHI Program Advisory Committee
- Data and Safety Monitoring Board
- Project Offices and Participating NIH Institutes
- Management Committee
- Executive Committee
    - Intervention Subcommittee
        - HRT Working Group
        - DM Working Group
        - CaD Working Group
    - Morbidity and Mortality Subcommittee
        - Cardiovascular Events Working Group
        - Cancer Events Working Group
        - Fracture Events Working Group
        - Other Age-Related Events Working Group
    - Operations Subcommittee
        - Recruitment and Retention Working Group
        - Training and Certification
        - Clinic Operations
        - Data Management
        - Laboratory Operations
    - Behavioral Subcommittee
        - Assessment Working Group
        - Retention Working Group
    - Special Populations Subcommittee
    - Observational Study Subcommittee
        - Cardiovascular Working Group
        - Cancer Working Group
        - Osteoporosis Working Group
    - Publications and Presentations Subcommittee
    - Design and Analysis Subcommittee
- Investigators Committee

H

NIH-Sponsored Women's Health Studies

The committee asked NIH to provide information about other studies of women's health within NIH. The following charts were developed from the documents provided by the various institutes.

Two charts were developed. The first contains those studies that are funded by more than one institute; the second includes those studies that are single-institute funded.

Those studies marked with an asterisk (*) do not necessarily focus on women, however NIH included them in the response regarding "Women's Health Studies." Abbreviations are as follows:

NHLBI	National Heart, Lung, and Blood Institute
NCI	National Cancer Institute
NIDDK	National Institute of Diabetes and Digestive and Kidney Diseases
NINDS	National Institute of Neurological Disorders and Stroke
NIAMS	National Institute of Arthritis and Musculoskeletal and Skin Diseases
NIDR	National Institute Dental Research
NIAAA	National Institute on Alcohol Abuse and Alcoholism
ORMH	Office for Research on Minority Health

TABLE H-1 WOMEN'S HEALTH STUDIES WITH MULTI-INSTITUTE FUNDING

Study Title	Contributing Institutes	Estimate of Costs by Institute ($)	Period of Study	Number of Subjects
Women's Health Trial: Feasibility Study in Minority Populations	NCI NHLBI NIDR	12,300,000 1,106,000 300,000 13,706,000	2 years	2,250
WHT Feasibility Study in Minority Populations: Salivary Study	NIDR (same as above)	300,000 (part of above)	2 years (same as above period)	200 (part of above sample)
Postmenopausal Estrogen/Progestin Interventions (PEPI)	NHLBI NICHD NIAMS NIA NIDDK	15,187,000 3,535,355 2,025,000 578,000 535,000 21,860,355	10 years	875
Breast Cancer Prevention Trial - Tamoxifen	NCI NHLBI NIAMS	65,820,000 7,931,000 2,136,000 75,887,000	7 years	16,000
Study of Osteoporotic Fractures	NIAMS NIA	32,489,000 14,615,191 47,104,191	11 years	9,700
Efficacy of Estrogen in Hyperprolactinemic Amenorrhea	NIDDK ORWH	1,043,032 NA 1,043,032	5 years	100
Membrous Lupus Nephropathy	NIDDK NCI	1,257,000 NA 1,257,000	9 years	16 to date (75% female)
Combination Radioiodine and Adriamycin for Follicular Thyroid Carcinoma	NIDDK NCI	1,499,000 NA 1,499,000	6 years	22 to date (75% female)
Vitamin E, Betacarotene and Aspirin in Women	NCI NHLBI	8,474,728 8,348,000 16,822,728	5 years	40,000
Long-Term Outcome of Obesity Treatment in Minority Women	NIDDK ORMH	3,534,011	6 years	600

APPENDIX H

TABLE H-2 WOMEN'S HEALTH STUDIES FUNDED BY SINGLE INSTITUTES

Study Title	Contributing Institute	Estimate of Cost ($)	Period of Study	Number of Subjects
Low Fat Diet and Breast Cancer Reccurrence	NCI	6,729,000	9 years	2,000
Carotene and Retinol Efficiency Trial	NCI	24,707,000+	13 years	17,000 (45% female)
A Dietary Study of the Recurrence of Large Bowel Adenomatoris Polyps	NCI	35,025,000	7 years	2,000 (30% female)
Screening Trial for Prostate, Lung, Colorectal, and Ovarian Cancer	NCI	74,517,000	16 years	148,000 (50% female)
Treatment Strategies for Osteoporosis	NIDDK	380,370	3 years	80
Ursodeoxycholate-Methotrexate for Primary Biliary Cirrhosis Clinical Trial	NIDDK	3,330,368	6 years	NA
Human Zinc Deficiency (MCH)	NIDDK	2,804,751	14 years	80
Low Fat Ad Libitum Diet and Weight Loss	NIDDK	617,246	3 years	118
Biosynthesis, Glycosylation, and Action of Thyrotropin: Clinical Trials of Recombinant TSH	NIDDK	2,008,000	3 years	35 (% female NA)
Obesity Treatment: Self-Management vs. Dependence Models	NIDDK	653,062	3 years	240
Modification of Director and Renal Disease*	NIDDK	59,020,000	10 years	855
Cardiovascular Health Study	NHLBI	63,370,000	6 years	5,201 (43% female)
Women's Health Study	NHLBI	8,348,000	5 years	41,600
Trial of Antioxidant Therapy of Cardiovascular Disease in Women (part of WHS)	NHLBI	3,122,000	5 years	8,000
Nurses's Health Study	NHLBI	2,762,000	13 years	121,700
Calcium for Preeclampsia Prevention	NHLBI	2,000,000	3 years	4,500
Cardiovascular Risk Factors and Menopause	NHLBI	2,207,000	4 years	550
Maintenance Psychotherapy in Recurrent Depression	NHLBI	3,800,000	5 years	180
Atherosclerosis Risk in Communities*	NHLBI	102,689,000	14 years	16,000 (% female NA)
NHLBI Growth and Health Study	NHLBI	16,645,000	9 years	2,379
Estrogen Effects on Cognition in Turner Syndrome	NINDS	1,209,014	9 years	2,379

continued on next page

TABLE H-2 Continued

Study Title	Contributing Institute	Estimate of Cost ($)	Period of Study	Number of Subjects
Women's Estrogen for Stroke Trial	NINDS	5,205,657	5 years	652
Genetic Epidemiology of Epilepsy*	NINDS	600,000	6 years	2,501 (46% female)
Incidence and Prevalence of Epilepsy*	NINDS	800,000	6 years	3,000 (50% female)
Rochester Diabetic Neuropathy Study	NINDS	3,744,698	9 years	380 (50% female)
Felbamage Concentration Response Trial*	NINDS	3,922,358	2 years	140 (50% female)
Genetic Epidemiology of Familial Epilepsy*	NINDS	1,449,561	10 years	340 (50% female)
Rectal Diazepam in Acute Repetitive Seizures*	NINDS	3,034,621	3 years	144 (47% female)
Remacemide Inpatience Seizure Evaluation Trial* (RISE)	NINDS	1,741,641	3 years	60 (33% female)
Control Study of Value of BMT for Storage Diseases*	NINDS	2,196,210	5 years	165 (50% female)
National Acute Spinal Cord Injury Study*	NINDS	6,609,929	17 years	495 (15% female)
Stroke Prevention in Atrial Fibrillation*	NINDS	14,799,368	9 years	3,400 (35% female)
Warfarin Aspirin Recurrent Stroke Study*	NINDS	25,875,696	5 years	1,920 (% female NA)
Brain Resuscitation Clinical Trial*	NINDS	3,379,284	14 years	2,500 (33% female)
North American Carotid Endarterectomy Trial*	NINDS	22,461,790	11 years	2,800 (% female NA)
Randomizes Trial of Tirilizad in Acute Stroke*	NINDS	1,124,130	2 years	700 (% female NA)
Phase II-B Randomized Controlled Study of Tissue Plasminogen Activator for Acute Ischemic Stroke*	NINDS	6,921,909	4 years	400 (% female NA)
Randomized Trial of ORG 10172 in Acute Ischemic Stroke and Data Management Center*	NINDS	9,532,046	5 years	1,800 (40% female)
Asymptomatic Carotid Artery Stenosis Collaborative Study*	NINDS	13,389,265	11 years	1,500 (35% female)
Studies of the Natural History and Response to Therapy in Multiple Sclerosis Using MRI*	NINDS	2,408,919	NA	38 (66% female)

APPENDIX H

TABLE H-2 Continued

Study Title	Contributing Institute	Estimate of Cost ($)	Period of Study	Number of Subjects
New alcohol problems and disorder: 11 year ECA follow-up*	NIAAA	311,680	3 years	867 (62% female)
Biological markers of alcohol consumption among women	NIAAA	67,486	NA	60
Secondary prevention of alcohol problems in women	NIAAA	147,259	2 years	NA (100% female)
Alcohol use among teenagers and infant outcome	NIAAA	126,829	NA	600
Effect of prenatal alcohol use on pediatric outcome	NIAAA	82,088	9 years	650
Neuroendocrine effects of alcohol on puberty*	NIAAA	135,866	NA	NA
Alcohol effects in postmenopausal women	NIAAA	240,368	NA	NA
Fetal alcohol exposure and female reproductive function*	NIAAA	210,781	NA	NA
Impact of labeling and education on antenatal drinking	NIAAA	169,689	NA	14,500
Fetal alcohol exposure -- From mechanism to prevention: protecting the next pregnancy*	NIAAA	186,102	NA	NA
Biological risk factors in relatives of alcoholic women	NIAAA	328,648	NA	NA
Hb-associated acetaldehyde -- A marker of fetal alcohol exposure*	NIAAA	57,211	NA	NA
Alcoholism and family interaction*	NIAAA	475,739	NA	300 (17% female)
Hispanic drinking and intra-family violence*	NIAAA	699,615	NA	800 (% female NA)
Genetic epidemiology -- Alcohol abuse in eating disorders	NIAAA	399,993	NA	147
A twin/family study of alcohol dependence in women	NIAAA	157,151	2 years	2,503 (app 70% female)
Alcohol use and HIV-related risky sex among adolescents*	NIAAA	110,486	5 years	2,676 (50% female)
Frequent heavy drinking and marital violence in newlyweds*	NIAAA	194,716	1 year	4,000 (50% female)
Experimental study of alcohol and marital aggression*	NIAAA	145,044	NA	440 (50% female)
Alcoholism and family history in women	NIAAA	174,599	NA	60
A twin study of female alcoholism and related disorders	NIAAA	762,450	App 20 years	2,400 (75% female)

TABLE H-2 Continued

Study Title	Contributing Institute	Estimate of Cost ($)	Period of Study	Number of Subjects
Family history of alcoholism and premenstrual symptoms	NIAAA	165,104	1 year	NA
Biobehavioral studies of alcohol problems in women	NIAAA	141,098	NA	NA
Alcohol and the menstrual cycle -- Biobehavioral studies	NIAAA	355,400	NA	NA
Mother's alcohol problems and children's victimization*	NIAAA	305,567	NA	App 1,000 (50% female)
Alcohol, breathing, and sleep -- Age and gender effects*	NIAAA	166,745	NA	NA
Cognitive and psychosocial recovery in alcoholic subtypes*	NIAAA	181,903	2 years	240 (50% female)
Longitudinal twin-family studies -- Use and abuse of alcohol*	NIAAA	298,897	5 years	12,500 (% female NA)
Problem drinking by future MDs*	NIAAA	190,951	NA	NA
Drinking, drug use and unsafe sex among gay and bisexual couples*	NIAAA	180,414	NA	NA
Maternal alcohol and lactational immune transfer	NIAAA	194,052	NA	NA
Interpersonal skills of adult children of alcoholics*	NIAAA	103,300	NA	240 (% female NA)
Dietary ethanol and initiation of DMBA tumorigenesis	NIAAA	124,602	NA	NA (100% female)
Characteristics of homeless women and their children*	NIAAA	301,844	NA	1,200 (% female NA)
Neurobehavioral aspects of fetal alcohol exposure*	NIAAA	895,954	NA	NA
Health beliefs and alcohol use in pregnant women	NIAAA	79,649	NA	200
Psychosocial correlates of adolescent driving behavior*	NIAAA	225,156	NA	5,000
Alcohol and stress -- Interactive effects*	NIAAA	123,328	NA	NA
Problem drinking in women -- A national survey follow-up	NIAAA	456,729	10 years	NA
Effects of alcohol in human ovarian cell function	NIAAA	168,224	NA	NA
Time-dependent effect of alcohol on spontaneous abortion	NIAAA	34,560	NA	5,300
Vulnerability factors and adolescent drinking*	NIAAA	172,191	2 years	3,190 (% female NA)
Behavioral risk for AIDS among alcoholics*	NIAAA	215,327	NA	1,500 (% female NA)
Children of alcoholics risk in young adults -- A longitudinal sibling design*	NIAAA	143,713	NA	12,686 (% female NA)
Primary care alcohol screens -- Patient sex and ethnicity*	NIAAA	74,750	2 years	1,350 (66% female)

I

NIH Cost and FTE Summary for Vanguard Clinical Centers

COST AND FTE SUMMARY
FOR VHI VANGUARD CLINICS, AS AWARDED
PERIOD OF PERFORMANCE: 12.5 YEARS
AVERAGE TOTAL COST: $10,497,597
AVERAGE TOTAL FTEs: 119.10
PREPARED 7/22/93
COMPILED BY MIKE WALKER AND DONNA WINTERS

	FTE	YEAR 01	FTE	YEAR 02	FTE	YEAR 03	FTE	YEAR 04	FTE	YEAR 05	FTE	YEAR 06
DIRECT LABOR												
Professional Level:	1.51	$85,123	1.76	$99,446	1.85	$105,640	1.78	$106,824	1.62	$96,326	1.52	$101,668
Other Staff:	5.32	$137,792	7.96	$235,072	7.53	$253,343	7.94	$257,491	6.36	$212,319	6.03	$216,666
Contributed:	0.23		0.24		0.34		0.31		0.23		0.23	
Total FTEs:	7.06		9.96		9.72		10.03		8.21		7.77	
DIRECT LABOR TOTAL:		$222,915		$334,518		$358,983		$364,315		$308,645		$318,334
FRINGE BENEFITS:		$54,923		$82,829		$90,360		$91,693		$78,438		$73,757
CONSULTANTS:	0.05	$2,279	0.03	$2,338	0.03	$2,463	0.05	$2,250	0.01	$756	0.01	$518
EQUIPMENT:		$77,575		$6,006		$4,489		$3,698		$3,366		$63,480
SUPPLIES:		$27,018		$26,298		$27,662		$26,262		$18,525		$18,476
TRAVEL:		$15,296		$12,745		$13,986		$14,305		$13,336		$13,556
LAB TESTS/PROCEDURES:		$17,482		$39,803		$61,805		$66,431		$59,245		$60,344
ALTERATIONS AND RENOVATIONS:		$1,138		$0		$0		$0		$0		$0
OTHER DIRECT COSTS:		$57,566		$77,552		$78,491		$71,127		$63,073		$66,348
SUBCONTRACT(S):												
LABOR: PROFESSIONAL:	0.32	$13,087	0.31	$14,886	0.35	$15,652	0.27	$16,626	0.17	$10,638	0.16	$10,277
STAFF:	1.18	$22,117	1.38	$38,902	1.38	$40,529	1.16	$37,866	1.17	$31,071	1.02	$36,616
CONTRIBUTED:	0.01		0.01		0.01		0.01		0.01		0.01	
FRINGE:		$4,664		$6,661		$6,984		$27,185		$21,904		$23,303
CONSULTANTS:	0.00	$0	0.00	$0	0.00	$0	0.00	$0	0.00	$0		$0
EQUIPMENT:		$0		$0		$0		$0		$0		$0
SUPPLIES:		$605		$1,390		$1,783		$1,847		$1,648		$1,693
TRAVEL:		$818		$660		$756		$750		$670		$679
LAB COSTS:		$2,923		$8,173		$12,413		$14,643		$13,246		$13,389
ALTERATIONS/REN.:		$0		$0		$0		$0		$0		$0
OTHER DIRECT:		$4,913		$8,787		$9,514		$6,239		$3,443		$5,803
INDIRECT COSTS:		$11,368		$22,399		$22,744		$20,961		$17,709		$17,724
TOTAL SUBCONTRACTS:	1.52	$60,495	1.70	$101,858	1.74	$110,356	1.44	$126,116	1.35	$100,328	1.19	$109,484
TOTAL DIRECT COST:		$536,685		$683,947		$748,594		$766,196		$645,712		$724,297
INDIRECT COST :		$122,765		$164,179		$176,960		$172,381		$147,486		$146,448
TOTAL COST (INDIRECT + DIRECT)	8.62	$659,450	11.69	$848,126	11.50	$925,554	11.52	$938,578	9.57	$793,199	8.97	$870,745

FTE	YEAR 07	FTE	YEAR 08	FTE	YEAR 09	FTE	YEAR 10	FTE	YEAR 11	FTE	YEAR 12	FTE	YEAR 13	TOTAL
1.44	$104,709	1.50	$109,054	1.51	$113,485	1.50	$108,878	1.50	$114,099	1.45	$124,674	0.69	$38,845	$1,308,770
5.81	$220,604	5.69	$225,837	5.14	$235,492	4.91	$246,061	5.64	$257,838	5.64	$275,090	1.74	$42,650	$2,816,254
0.19		0.19		0.19		0.20		0.19		0.20		0.14		98.22 (FTEs)
7.45		7.38		6.85		6.61		7.33		7.28		2.57		
	$325,313		$334,891		$348,977		$354,939		$371,937		$399,764		$81,495	$4,125,024
	$81,176		$83,602		$87,014		$90,844		$95,073		$98,085		$19,614	$1,027,407
0.01	$541	0.01	$572	0.01	$591	0.01	$617	0.01	$645	0.01	$673	0.003	$205	$14,448
	$3,051		$1,783		$1,661		$2,189		$11,168		$1,615		$1,558	$181,639
	$16,037		$15,205		$15,860		$16,538		$16,167		$16,132		$2,884	$243,063
	$13,822		$13,056		$14,466		$15,311		$15,985		$17,057		$6,464	$179,384
	$64,051		$56,559		$62,757		$57,682		$64,970		$59,226		$33	$670,387
	$0		$0		$0		$0		$0		$0		$0	$1,138
	$62,994		$64,078		$66,191		$76,734		$92,685		$85,191		$28,879	$890,909
														$0
0.14	$10,459	0.16	$10,792	0.16	$11,246	0.16	$11,663	0.16	$12,096	0.16	$12,545	0.05	$3,106	$153,075
1.00	$37,745	0.91	$37,386	0.90	$37,523	0.89	$38,596	0.89	$40,193	5.83	$43,623	0.27	$7,410	$449,593
0.01	$0		$0	0.01	$0	0.01	$0	0.01	$0	0.01	$0	0.00	$0	$0
	$24,172		$28,198		$25,353		$5,594		$5,820		$6,335		$1,502	
	$0		$0		$0		$0		$0		$0		$0	$0
	$1,607		$1,462		$1,463		$1,491		$1,527		$1,560		$91	$18,166
	$705		$732		$759		$789		$819		$852		$240	$9,210
	$13,137		$12,963		$13,146		$13,286		$13,461		$13,596		$0	$144,376
	$0		$0		$0		$0		$0		$0		$0	$0
	$3,188		$1,734		$3,216		$3,315		$3,415		$3,524		$525	$57,616
	$18,787		$19,109		$19,711		$20,405		$40,061		$22,254		$3,185	$256,416
1.15	$109,799	1.07	$112,375	1.08	$112,418	1.06	$95,138	1.06	$117,393	6.00	$104,289	0.32	$16,059	$1,276,108
	$676,783		$682,121		$709,934		$709,992		$766,024		$782,032		$157,189	$7,333,399
	$150,386		$151,340		$159,773		$164,178		$174,045		$177,634		$35,384	$1,942,960 TOTAL COST
8.61	$827,169	8.45	$833,461	7.93	$869,707	7.68	$874,170	8.40	$960,068	13.28	$904,797	2.89	$192,574	$10,497,597

FTEs: 119.10

J
NIH Power Calculations[1]

---

[1]Reprinted with permission from the June 28, 1993 WHI Protocol, pages 77-83.

(i) ERT versus Control: Coronary Heart Disease.

Average follow-up (y)	Intervention effect (%)	Percentage cases		Power (%) Total sample size		
		Control	ERT (or PERT)	20,000	25,000	30,000
6	25	3.26	2.71	50	59	67
	30	3.26	2.62	66	76	83
	35	3.25	2.49	80	88	93
9	25	5.03	4.16	69	79	86
	30	5.02	3.97	85	92	96
	35	5.01	3.79	94	98	99

(ia) PERT versus Control: Coronary Heart Disease.

Average follow-up (y)	Intervention effect (%)	Percentage cases		Power (%) Total sample size		
		Control	PERT	20,000	25,000	30,000
6	25	3.26	2.71	48	57	65
	30	3.26	2.60	64	74	82
	35	3.25	2.49	79	87	92
9	25	5.03	4.16	67	77	84
	30	5.02	3.97	84	91	95
	35	5.01	3.79	94	97	99

(ii) ERT versus Control: Combined Fractures.
(The percentage of cases and the powers in this table are based upon our original age distribution assumptions, i.e., 50-59, 60-69, 70-79 year olds enter in the ratio 2:2:1, and hence are conservative estimates.)

Average follow-up (y)	Intervention effect (%)	Percentage cases		Power (%) Total sample size		
		Control	ERT	20,000	25,000	30,000
6	25	5.84	4.86	79	87	92
	30	5.84	4.66	92	96	98
	35	5.83	4.46	98	99	>99
9	25	8.85	7.31	94	97	99
	30	8.84	6.99	99	>99	>99
	35	8.82	6.66	>99	>99	>99

(iia) ERT versus Control: Combined Fractures.
(The percentage of cases and the powers in this table are based upon our original age distribution assumptions, i.e., 50-59, 60-69, 70-79 year olds enter in the ratio 2:2:1, and hence are conservative estimates.)

Average follow-up (y)	Intervention effect (%)	Percentage cases		Power (%) Total sample size		
		Control	PERT	20,000	25,000	30,000
6	25	5.84	4.86	77	85	91
	30	5.84	4.66	90	95	98
	35	5.83	4.46	98	99	>99
9	25	8.85	7.31	93	97	99
	30	8.84	6.99	99	>99	>99
	35	8.82	6.66	>99	>99	>99

(iii) ERT versus Control: Hip Fractures.

Average follow-up (y)	Intervention effect (%)	Percentage cases		Power (%) Total sample size		
		Control	ERT	20,000	25,000	30,000
6	25	2.34	1.94	41	49	56
	30	2.34	1.86	55	65	73
	35	2.33	1.77	70	79	86
9	25	3.91	3.22	62	71	79
	30	3.90	3.07	78	87	92
	35	3.89	2.92	90	95	98

(iiia) PERT versus Control: Hip Fractures.

Average follow-up (y)	Intervention effect (%)	Percentage cases		Power (%) Total sample size		
		Control	PERT	20,000	25,000	30,000
6	25	2.34	1.94	39	47	54
	30	2.34	1.86	54	63	71
	35	2.33	1.77	68	77	84
9	25	3.91	3.22	60	69	77
	30	3.90	3.07	76	85	91
	35	3.89	2.92	88	94	97

(iv) ERT versus Control: Breast Cancer.

Average follow-up (y)	Increase due to ERT (%)	Percentage Cases		Power (%) Total Sample Size		
		Control	ERT	20,000	25,000	30,000
6	20	2.07	2.25	13	15	17
	30	2.08	2.35	23	28	32
9	20	3.04	3.40	27	33	38
	30	3.05	3.60	52	61	69
14	20	4.5	5.17	52	62	70
	30	4.53	5.54	85	92	96

(iva) PERT versus Control: Breast Cancer.

Average follow-up (y)	Increase due to PERT (%)	Percentage Cases		Power (%) Total Sample Size		
		Control	ERT	20,000	25,000	30,000
6	20	2.07	2.25	12	14	16
	30	2.08	2.35	22	27	31
9	20	3.04	3.40	26	32	37
	30	3.05	3.60	50	60	67
14	20	4.50	5.17	51	60	68
	30	4.53	5.54	83	91	95

(i) Dietary Modification: Breast Cancer.

Average follow-up (y)	Intervention effect (%)	Percentage of cases		Power (%) Sample size		
		Control	Intervention	42,000	48,000	54,000
6	11	2.05	1.89	25	28	31
	12	2.05	1.87	32	35	39
	14	2.05	1.85	39	44	48
9	11	2.92	2.61	58	63	69
	12	2.92	2.57	70	75	80
	14	2.92	2.52	81	86	89

(ii) Dietary Modification: Colorectal Cancer.

Average follow-up (y)	Intervention effect (%)	Percentage of cases		Power (%) Sample size		
		Control	Intervention	42,000	48,000	54,000
6	18	1.07	0.93	33	37	41
	20	1.07	0.92	40	45	49
	22	1.07	0.91	47	52	57
9	18	1.61	1.32	77	83	87
	20	1.61	1.29	86	90	93
	22	1.60	1.25	92	95	97

(iii) Dietary Modification: Coronary Heart Disease.

Average follow-up (y)	Intervention effect	Percentage of cases		Power (%) Sample size		
		Control	Intervention	42,000	48,000	54,000
6	11	3.04	2.72	48	53	58
	12	3.03	2.67	58	64	69
	14	3.02	2.63	68	74	79
9	11	4.62	4.15	62	67	72
	12	4.60	4.08	72	78	83
	14	4.58	4.00	82	86	90

(i) Calcium/Vitamin D versus Control: Hip Fractures

Average Follow-up (y)	Intervention effect (%)	Percentage cases Control	Percentage cases Calcium/ Vitamin D	Power (%) Total sample size 25,000	35,000	45,000
5	25	1.88	1.58	53	67	78
	30	1.88	1.51	69	83	91
	35	1.88	1.45	83	93	97
8	25	3.35	2.76	81	92	97
	30	3.34	2.64	93	98	>99
	35	3.34	2.51	98	>99	>99

(ii) Calcium/Vitamin D versus Control: Combined Fractures

(The percentages of cases and powers in this table are based upon our original age distribution assumptions i.e., 50-59, 60-69, 70-79 year olds enter in the ratio 2.2.1 and hence are conservative estimates.)

Average Follow-up (y)	Intervention effect (%)	Percentage cases Control	Percentage cases Calcium/ Vitamin D	Power (%) Total sample size 25,000	35,000	45,000
5	25	4.84	4.07	90	97	99
	30	4.84	3.91	98	>99	>99
	35	4.83	3.75	>99	>99	>99
8	25	7.85	6.49	99	>99	>99
	30	7.83	6.20	>99	>99	>99
	35	7.82	5.91	>99	>99	>99

(iii) Calcium/Vitamin D versus Control: Colorectal Cancer

Average Follow-up (y)	Intervention effect (%)	Percentage cases Control	Percentage cases Calcium/ Vitamin D	Power (%) Total sample size 25,000	35,000	45,000
5	18	0.86	0.76	17	23	28
	20	0.86	0.75	20	27	33
	22	0.86	0.74	24	31	38
8	25	1.42	1.17	52	66	77
	30	1.42	1.15	60	75	85
	35	1.42	1.12	69	83	91

K

Women's Health Initiative Clinical Coordinating Center and Vanguard Clinical Centers Principal Investigators

Clinical Coordinating Center

Ross L. Prentice, Ph.D.
Fred Hutchinson Cancer
 Research Center
Seattle, Washington

Vanguard Clinical Centers

Gregory L. Burke, M.D., M.S.
The Bowman Gray
School of Medicine
Winston-Salem, North Carolina

JoAnn Manson, M.D., Dr.P.H.
Brigham and Women's Hospital
Boston

Maurizio Trevisan, M.D., M.S.
State University of New York,
 Buffalo

Albert Oberman, M.D.*
University of Alabama
Birmingham

Thomas E. Moon, Ph.D.
University of Arizona

W. Dallas Hall, M.D.*
Emory University School of Medicine

Maureen Henderson, M.D.
Fred Hutchinson Cancer Research Center
Seattle, Washington

Annlouise R. Assaf, Ph.D.
The Memorial Hospital
Pawtucket, Rhode Island

Philip Greenland, M.D.
Northwestern University Medical School

John A. Robbins, M.D.
University of California, Davis

Robert D. Langer, M.D., M.P.H.*
University of California, San Diego

*These Vanguard Clinical Centers will recruit primarily minority populations.

Norman L. Lasser, M.D.
University of Medicine and
 Dentistry of New Jersey

Robert Wallace, MD
University of Iowa

Richard H. Grimm, M.D.
University of Minnesota
 Medical School

Lewis H. Kuller, M.D.
University of Pittsburgh

William B. Applegate, M.D.
University of Tennessee,
 Memphis

L
Abbreviations and Acronyms

CaD	Calcium and vitamin D supplementation
CCC	Clinical Coordinating Center
CHD	Coronary heart disease
CPS	Community Prevention Study
CT	Clinical Trial
CVD	Cardiovascular disease
DM	Dietary modification
DSMB	Data Safety and Monitoring Board
ERT	Estrogen replacement therapy
HDL-C	High-density lipoprotein cholesterol
HRT	Hormone replacement therapy
IOM	Institute of Medicine
LDL-C	Low-density lipoprotein cholesterol
NAS	National Academy of Sciences
NCI	National Cancer Institute
NIH	National Institutes of Health
OPR	Objective Prescheduled Reassessment
OS	Observational Study
PEPI	Postmenopausal Estrogen Progestin Interventions Trial
PERT	Progestin-plus-estrogen replacement therapy
PI	Principal investigator
SES	Socioeconomic status
WHI	Women's Health Initiative

M

Committee and Staff Biographies

Lucile L. Adams-Campbell, Ph.D.
Dr. Adams-Campbell holds three positions at Howard University in Washington, D.C. She is currently the Associate Director of the Division of Epidemiology and Cancer Control and Associate Professor of Oncology at the Howard University College of Medicine. She is also a Graduate Associate Professor in the Department of Physiology and Biophysics at the Howard University Graduate School of Arts and Sciences. Dr. Adams-Campbell received her Ph.D. in Epidemiology from the University of Pittsburgh in 1983, where she was a Post Doctorate Fellow in Cardiovascular Disease. Dr. Adams-Campbell is a member of several professional organizations, and has served on the boards of the Association of Black Cardiologists, the Society of Behavioral Medicine, SER, and the Society for Analysis of African-American Public Health Issues. Dr. Adams-Campbell has been awarded many academic and professional honors, the most recent being the Searle Distinguished Research Award in 1992.

Abdelmonen A. Afifi, Ph.D.
Dr. Afifi is the Dean of the School of Public Health at the University of California at Los Angeles, after serving as Head of the Biostatistics Division. He completed his Ph.D. in Statistics in 1965 at the University of California at Berkeley, and an M.S. degree at the University of Chicago in 1962. Dr. Afifi was a Guest Scholar at the International Institute of Applied Systems Analysis in Laxenburg, Austria. Dr. Afifi is a member of several scientific organizations, including APHA, the Institute of Mathematical Statistics, the American Statistics Association, and the Biometric Society. Dr. Afifi reviews articles for many scientific journals, and is an associate editor for *Computation Statistics and Data Analysis, Alzheimer Disease and Associated Disorders - An International Journal,* and *Journal of Health Care for the Poor and Underserved.* Dr. Afifi is also the recipient of many awards, and most recently received the Lowell Reed Award for Excellence in Teaching and Research from the Statistics Section of the American Public Health Association.

Kelly D. Brownell, Ph.D.
At Yale University, Dr. Brownell is a Professor of Psychology, Professor of Epidemiology and Public Health, and the Co-Director of the Yale Center for Eating and Weight Disorders. Earlier, he was a professor in the Department of Psychiatry and the University of Pennsylvania School of Medicine. In 1977, Dr. Brownell received his Ph.D. in

Clinical Psychology from Rutgers University, after completing an internship at Brown University. Dr. Brownell has received numerous awards, including the Outstanding Academic Book Award from the American Library Association for *Handbook of Behavioral Medicine for Women*. His paper on "Understanding and Preventing Relapse" published in the *American Psychologist* was identified as one of the ten most frequently cited papers in psychology. Dr. Brownell has served as President of the Society of Behavioral Medicine, the Division of Health Psychology of the American Psychological Association, and the Association for the Advancement of Behavior Therapy, and has served on the Board of Directors of other organizations including the North American Association for the Study of Obesity and the Society for the Experimental Analysis of Behavior.

Gary R. Cutter, Ph.D.

Since 1991 Dr. Cutter has been the President of Pythagoras, Inc. Prior to this he was Chairman, Biostatistics and Information Systems at St. Jude Children's Research Hospital and prior to that was a Professor in the Schools of Medicine and Public Health at the University of Alabama at Birmingham. Dr. Cutter received his M.S. in 1971 and his Ph.D. in 1974 in Biometry from the University of Texas School of Public Health in Houston. Dr. Cutter has been involved with and directed numerous coordinating centers of multi-center research, the most recent being the Umbilical Artery Catheter Placement Study, the Coronary Artery Risk Development in Young Adults study, and the Contact Lens Ocular Complications Study. Dr. Cutter is a current member of several government advisory committees including the Data and Safety Monitoring Committees for the Hydroxyurea in the Treatment of Sickle Cell Disease; the Diabetes Control and Complications Trial and its Biostatistics Monitoring Group; and the Dietary Effects on Lipoproteins and Thrombogenic Activity Study. He serves as an administrator as Chairman NHLBI Special Emphasis Panel and is a member of the study section, the NHLBI Clinical Trials Review Committee. He is a member of the Research Committee of the American Sports Medicine Institute and serves on several committees for various professional associations.

John W. Farquhar, M.D.

Dr. Farquhar is the Director of the Stanford Center for Research in Disease Prevention, and is the C.F. Rehnborg Professor of Disease Prevention, and a Professor of Medicine and of Health Research and Policy at the Stanford University School of Medicine. He received his M.D. in 1952 from the University of California School of Medicine at San Francisco. Dr. Farquhar completed a residency in medicine at the University of Minnesota School of Medicine, and returned to San Francisco as a USPHS Postdoctoral Fellow in Cardiology. Dr. Farquhar took a sabbatical leave at the London School of Hygiene and Tropical Medicine in the Department of Epidemiology and Medical Statistics in 1968-69. Dr. Farquhar has received many academic honors, including the American Heart Association's Research Achievement Award in 1992. He was elected to membership in the Institute of Medicine, National Academy of Sciences in 1978.

COMMITTEE AND STAFF BIOGRAPHIES

Marion J. Finkel, M.D. (*Chair*)

Dr. Finkel is the Vice President of Drug Registration and Regulatory Affairs of Sandoz Pharmaceuticals. She received her M.D. from Chicago Medical School in 1952, completed a Rotating Internship at the Jersey City Medical Center in 1952-1953, and did her residency in Internal Medicine at the Cumberland Hospital (1953) and Bellevue Hospital N.Y.U. Post Graduate Medical Division (1954-1956). Dr. Finkel worked with the Food and Drug Administration from 1963 to 1985, beginning as Medical Officer in the Bureau of Medicine and serving as Director of the Division of Metabolism and Endocrine Drugs, Deputy Director, Bureau of Drugs, Director of the Office of Scientific Evaluation, and Director of the Office of Orphan Products Development. Dr. Finkel is active with numerous professional organizations. Dr. Finkel has received many Federal awards, including a presidential award, public health service awards and FDA awards. She has published and presented over 100 papers.

Penny M. Kris-Etherton, Ph.D., R.D.

Dr. Kris-Etherton is Professor of Nutrition at The Pennsylvania State University. She received her M.S. degree in nutrition from Case Western Reserve University and became a Registered Dietitian in 1973. She was awarded her Ph.D. in Human Nutrition (supporting field: biochemistry and physiology) in 1978 from the University of Minnesota. As a Katherine McCormick Scholar, Dr. Kris-Etherton was a Postdoctoral Research Fellow at Stanford University in Lipid Metabolism. She was a Visiting Scholar at the Stanford Center for Research in Disease Prevention in 1986-1987, and a Visiting Scientist at the University of Hohenheim, West Germany, Institute of Biological Chemistry and Nutrition. From 1987 to 1991, Dr. Kris-Etherton served on the Arteriosclerosis, Hypertension and Lipid Metabolism Advisory Committee of the NIH, and participates in many professional activities. She has also served as a federal government consultant for NIH and NHLBI. Dr. Kris-Etherton has received many honors, and in 1991 received the Lederle Award for contributions to human nutrition research from the American Institute of Nutrition.

Jennifer L. Kelsey, Ph.D.

Dr. Kelsey is Chief of the Division of Epidemiology and Professor of Health Research and Policy at the Stanford University School of Medicine. Dr. Kelsey was awarded her Ph.D. in Epidemiology (chronic diseases) at Yale University in 1969. Dr. Kelsey is an active member of professional groups, and is currently on the editorial board for the *Journal of Bone and Mineral Research*, the Merck Scientific Advisory Committee for fellowships in clinical epidemiology, a series editor for the *Oxford Monographs in Epidemiology and Biostatistics*, and an editor for *Epidemiologic Reviews*. In 1991, Dr. Kelsey received the John Snow Award from the American Public Health Association for contributions to epidemiology.

D. Joanne Lynn, M.D.

Dr. Lynn is a Professor of Medicine and of Community and Family Medicine, Associate Director of the Center for the Aging, and a Senior Associate in the Center for the Evaluative Clinical Sciences at Dartmouth-Hitchcock Medical Center. Before moving to

Dartmouth, Dr. Lynn held various positions in geriatrics and health services research at The George Washington University in Washington, D.C. Dr. Lynn received her M.D. in 1974 from Boston University and completed her residency in Internal Medicine at The George Washington University. Dr. Lynn earned an M.A. in Philosophy and Social Policy in 1982. She is Co-Director of SUPPORT, the Study to Understand Prognosis and Performance for Outcomes and Risks of Treatments, and was Assistant Director of the President's Commission for the Study of Ethical Problems in Medicine and Biomedical and Behavioral Research. Dr. Lynn is active in several professional groups, including the American Hospital Association, Technical Panel on Biomedical Ethics; the American Geriatrics Society, Committees on Public Policy and Ethics and Board of Directors; and the Geriatrics and Gerontology Advisory Committee to the Department of Veterans Affairs.

Lynn Rosenberg, Sc.D.

Dr. Rosenberg is a Professor of Epidemiology at the School of Public Health and Assistant Director of the Slone Epidemiology Unit, both at the Boston University School of Medicine. In 1978 Dr. Rosenberg received her Sc.D. in Epidemiology. She also received an M.S. in Biostatistics from the Harvard School of Public Health, and an M.S. in Chemistry from Boston University, Graduate School of Chemistry. She was a National Science Foundation Fellow from 1960-1961. Dr. Rosenberg is active in several professional groups, including the Society for Epidemiologic Research, of which she was President in 1992, and acts as Associate Editor for the *American Journal of Epidemiology*.

Diane B. Stoy, Ed.D., R.N.

Dr. Stoy is the Operations Director of the Lipid Research Clinic at The George Washington University Medical Center in Washington, D.C. where she is also an Adjunct Assistant Professor in the Department of Health Care Sciences, and Legislative Director for the D.C. Cardiovascular and Renal Education Consortium. Dr. Stoy received her Ed.D. from The George Washington University in 1993 in Human Resources Development/Cross Cultural Studies, and completed her M.A. in Adult Education with distinction in 1983. Dr. Stoy received her Diploma in Nursing in 1966. As clinical director of one of the original Lipid Research Clinics she has directed numerous federally sponsored clinical trials, including the Coronary Primary Prevention Trial, the Postmenopausal Estrogen Progestin Interventions Trial, the Cholesterol Reduction in Senior Persons Study, as well as the Heart Estrogen-Progestin Replacement Therapy. Dr. Stoy is active in many professional organizations, including the American Heart Association, Council on Cardiovascular Nursing, and co-chair of the Interdisciplinary Professional Education Program; the American Public Health Association; the American Society for Health Education and Training; the International Society for Intercultural Education, Training and Research. Dr. Stoy is also a member of the NIH Task Force on the Recruitment and Retention of Women in Clinical Trials. She has served as a health care consultant on a variety of organizations within the federal government and private sectors, and has received numerous awards for her work in health education.

COMMITTEE AND STAFF BIOGRAPHIES

IOM Staff

Donna F. Allen

Donna F. Allen is the Project Assistant for the Committee to Review the NIH Women's Health Initiative. Mrs. Allen is a practiced meeting coordinator, and has acquired over twenty years of administrative, supervisory, and logistics experience in business administration and computer science. She is competent in a myriad of software and database maintenance tools. Prior to coming to the Institute of Medicine, she was the Administrative Assistant to the Computer Science and Telecommunications Board, National Research Council and has supported several other committees in her twelve years of service at the National Academy of Sciences. Mrs. Allen is working towards her degree in Business Administration.

Dana Hotra, M.H.S.

Dana Hotra is a Research Associate at the Institute of Medicine. She received her B.A. in anthropology at the University of California at Santa Barbara and her M.H.S. from the Department of Maternal and Child Health, The Johns Hopkins School of Hygiene and Public Health. Prior to joining the Institute of Medicine in 1991, she coordinated the Volunteer Program at the National Abortion Rights Action League in Washington, D.C. Ms. Hotra works on two projects at the Institute of Medicine: the Committee to Review the NIH Women's Health Initiative in the Food and Nutrition Board, and the Study of Female Morbidity and Mortality in Sub-Saharan Africa in the Division of International Health.

Felice H. LePar, A.B.

Felice LePar was the Research Assistant for the Committee to Review the NIH Women's Health Initiative from June through July 1993. She graduated in June 1992 from Princeton University with an A.B. with High Honors in Chemistry and a Certificate in Woodrow Wilson School of Public and International Affairs. Ms. Lepar held an internship in the Congressional Research Service and has interests in bioethics and women's health. She attends Harvard Medical School, and plans to study for an M.P.H. or M.P.P. after graduating in June 1996.

Valerie Petit Setlow, Ph.D.

Valerie Petit Setlow is Director of the Health Sciences Policy Division, Institute of Medicine, National Academy of Sciences. She received her B.S. from Xavier University of Louisiana in 1970 and her Ph.D. in Molecular Biology from The Johns Hopkins University in 1976. After Postdoctoral research at Mt. Sinai Hospital, New York, and NIH intramural laboratories, Dr. Setlow joined the National Institute of Arthritis, Diabetes, Digestive and Kidney Diseases successively as Special Assistant and Assistant Program Director for the Diabetes Research Program and then as Director of the Cystic Fibrosis Research Program. She served concurrently as Assistant to the Division Director of the Diabetes, Endocrinology and Metabolic Diseases Division for management and operations. Dr. Setlow later joined the Office of the Assistant Secretary for Health as a Senior Health Policy Analyst.

Subsequently, she joined the National AIDS Program Office (NAPO) as the NIH Desk Officer and then held increasingly responsible positions in NAPO; as the Director of the Policy Analysis and Coordination staff, as Deputy Director, and then as Acting Director of the office. Dr. Setlow is a member of the American Association for the Advancement of Science and the American Society for Biochemists and Molecular Biologists (ASBMB). Dr. Setlow is the recipient of a number of individual and group honors and awards from the Public Health Service.

Susan Thaul, Ph.D. *(Study Director)*

Serving as Study Director of the Committee to Review the NIH Women's Health Initiative has been Susan Thaul's first assignment at the Institute of Medicine, where she is also the Director of the National Forum on Health Statistics. She received a Ph.D. in epidemiology from Columbia University and an M.S. in health policy and management from Harvard University. Dr. Thaul most recently led the health staff of the U.S. Senate Committee on Veterans' Affairs, where she developed legislation in preventive health care and research, women's health care, sexual assault services and prevention, nurse and physician pay, and health effects of environmental hazards during military service. Earlier positions were with the Hospital Studies Program of what is now the Agency for Health Care Policy and Research, working on the costs of pediatric AIDS and the costs of hospital care for research subjects; the Harlem Hospital Prevention of Prematurity Project; and the NYC Health and Hospitals Corporation, where Dr. Thaul held successive positions leading to Associate Director of the NYC Emergency Medical Service.

Catherine E. Woteki, Ph.D., R.D.

Catherine E. Woteki is Director of the Institute of Medicine's Food and Nutrition Board. Prior to joining the IOM, she was Deputy Director of the Division of Health Examination Statistics, National Center for Health Statistics, U.S. Department of Health and Human Services. She has served in important health posts at the Office of Technology Assessment of the U.S. Congress and at the U.S. Department of Agriculture's Human Nutrition Information Service. Dr. Woteki is co-editor of the FNB publication, *Eat For Life: The Food and Nutrition Board's Guide to Reducing Your Risk of Chronic Disease*. She was a recipient of an IOM Distinguished Staff Award in 1991 and holds various honors from the Public Health Service, U.S. Department of Health and Human Services. Dr. Woteki currently serves as a member of the Council on Research of the American Dietetic Association, and on the editorial advisory board of the American Institute of Nutrition. Dr. Woteki holds a B.S. in Biology and Chemistry from Mary Washington College, Fredricksburg, Virginia; and M.S. and Ph.D. degrees in Human Nutrition from Virginia Polytechnic and State University, Blacksburg, Virginia.